10 0284216 2

EXPRESS
NEWSPAPERS

EXPRESS NEWSPAPERS

The Inside Story of a Turbulent Decade

ANDREW CAMERON

LONDON
HOUSE

First published in Great Britain in 2000 by
LONDON HOUSE
114 New Cavendish Street
London W1M 7FD

A catalogue record for this book is available
from the British Library

ISBN 1 902809 440

Edited and designed by DAG Publications Ltd, London.
Printed and bound by
Creative Print and Design (Wales)

CONTENTS

INTRODUCTION

A NUMBER OF BOOKS have been written about Fleet Street. These have mostly been by editors reflecting their roles in, and contributions to, the world of journalism, and their relationships with proprietors. In many, politics have featured significantly, reflecting a national newspaper editor's frequent contacts at high level amongst prime ministers, ministers and spin doctors.

The term 'Fleet Street' is essentially a generic term for national newspaper journalism. There is, however, another side to the story: the running of the companies that produce those newspapers.

It used to be said that there was 'always another funeral passing down Fleet Street' – newspaper failures happened with great frequency over the years. The industry lurched from crisis to crisis. 'Will we be next?' people would cry, as they submitted yet another massive wage claim. *The Empire News, The Sunday Graphic, The News Chronicle, Today, The Daily Sketch* and the *Evening News*, to name but a few, became casualties – and who remembers them today?

I wrote this book because Fleet Street and the industry giants who ran it and edited the newspapers are essentially of the past. The days when newspapers were the sole means of communication and comment in the land diminished increasingly rapidly from the early sixties, when television really began to get a grip on the population as its primary source of news and entertainment. Now the availability of information to the public has never been so prolific via the electronic media, which is itself only just beginning.

Regardless of where any industry is going, there are always lessons to be learned from the past. There are footsteps to follow and pitfalls to be avoided so future generations do not make the same mistakes. After all, who would have thought that after the First World War a further World War would have occurred within a mere twenty-one years? How many companies listed on the FT100 were around even fifty years ago? Were the mistakes their predecessors made concerning markets and people predictable? Lord Beaverbrook, when approached to invest in the early days of commercial television, famously replied: 'It's a passing fancy.' When companies are highly successful in their chosen field, everything seems rosy and the longer-term future may be considered to take care of itself. But history often has a way of repeating itself.

It is also worth considering the remark of one major industrialist who was asked why he spent such large sums of money supporting his top-selling brands. He replied that there is always somebody you may not yet have noticed coming up behind you and who will steal the crown jewels before you realise what has happened … and, when you do realise what has happened, it will be too late.

Newspapers for too long preached from ivory towers with ponderous leader columns. It took Rupert Murdoch to listen and to understand what people wanted and to embrace the new electronic media as part of the whole – print feeding off television and vice-versa, making a powerful combination to disseminate news and entertainment to the mass market, which had at one time been the sole prerogative of newspapers.

My long background in the industry, I believe, well qualifies me to comment. I started my career in the provinces, and by mid-career held senior management positions at Express Newspapers, which was in itself a microcosm of the industry. I have steered clear wherever possible of industry jargon, and I hope that this book gives the reader an insight into a unique industry.

The history of the newspaper industry is a story of individuals. How many other businesses write copy today, print tonight, and then the product becomes fish'n'chip paper by the end of the following morning? All that effort for a moment of fame (or infamy as the case may be) ...

Andrew Cameron, 2000

ACKNOWLEDGEMENTS

I extend my thanks to the following for sharing their memories: Alan Bellinger, Brian Hitchen, Leith McGrandle, Henry Mcrory, Ray Mills and Phil Rostron.

Andrew Cameron

1

A BEST KEPT SECRET

THE MERGER between United News & Media plc and MAI plc in the spring of 1996 was one of the best kept corporate secrets ever. Not a hint of the impending deal had reached the City. Yet, negotiations had been going on, followed by due diligence, for around six months prior to the formal announcement.

The predecessor of United News & Media, United Newspapers, had grown under David (Lord) Stevens from a sleepy £23 million turnover provincial newspaper company in the mid-1980s to a £950 million turnover multi-national by the mid-1990s. United's principal burden was Express Newspapers, publishers of the *Daily Express*, *Sunday Express* and *Daily Star*, which had been purchased from Fleet Holdings, the group demerged from Trafalgar House, in 1985.

United needed profits to meet City expectations, and a great deal of money was spent on replanting and redundancies following the Fleet Street revolution of the mid-1980s which followed the Thatcher/Tebbit laws on industrial relations, and Eddie Shah's use of these laws at Warrington in Lancashire. Every Fleet Street newspaper group jumped through the hoop created by these changes to modernise and reduce staff to realistic levels after generations of trade union domination of the newspaper industry

As managing director of the Express Group I knew only too well that the *Express* represented a big chunk of United's profitability. The pressure on bottom lines was extreme and United did not have the money to invest in the titles to make them competitive with their rivals. Compared with our competitors, the *Express* titles were badly under-funded where it really needed to count – paging, editorial and publicity.

Our newspapers were outgunned on all these fronts by highly professional publishers, not the least of whom was Lord Rothermere, a man with ink in his veins and a dynasty to protect. Add to this scenario the outbreak of the newspaper cover price war of the mid-1990s, led by Rupert Murdoch, and the results were predictable.

All we as a management could do was to control costs and try to manage the inevitable circulation decline. Sales of *Express* titles fell consistently and depressed the market value of the parent company, despite making £300 million of profit during my ten-year tenure as managing director. The City waited and watched the circulation figures closely.

The changes in cross-media ownership rules in 1996 made some of the United directors extremely nervous about the future independence of the company. Since United was not sufficiently big to make a major acquisition to ensure invulnerability, a merger was sought. A takeover of the Express Group became inevitable.

Part of the deal with MAI was that Lord ('call me Clive') Hollick, the Labour peer who was chairman of MAI, would become chief executive of the combined company and all divisions would report to him, with Lord Stevens remaining chairman. (The national newspapers had always reported directly to the chairman since Beaverbrook's day but, under the Hollick regime, this arrangement was to end.)

I met Hollick four times, two of them social. What I didn't know when I voted for the merger as a main board director of United News-papers was that my future and fate were also part of the deal.

Hollick sent for me at 8.45 on the morning of 3 May 1996. I had been up until the small hours of the morning with our lawyers hammering out a separate business deal and was hardly at my best when I confronted Hollick. My 24-year career in national newspapers ended in seconds. Hollick was nothing if not brief and brutal.

'I have decided to put together the national newspapers, regional newspapers and Link House magazines into one division, and I have appointed Stephen Grabiner to do the job. I expect you have had to do this many times. Perhaps you would like to see the personnel director? Oh, and could you be out of your office by the end of the day?'

Finis.

I had been managing director of Express Newspapers for ten years and spent a lifetime in newspaper management. I had witnessed the world of newspapers going through the most turbulent times in the history of Fleet Street.

This is the story of those years – warts, stings and all – by someone who really was on the inside.

*   *   *   *   *

I was born on 23 March 1943 in Scarborough. My father was a general practitioner who had set himself up – as part of the first group practice, prior to the birth of the National Health Service in 1948 – in the little town of Builth Wells, in beautiful mid-Wales.

My elder brother and I, at the age of eight, were sent to prep school in Shrewsbury, and then, in 1955, to public school – Denstone College, a nineteenth-century establishment of forbidding grey granite atop a hill near Uttoxeter in Staffordshire.

During holidays I was handyman and gofer at Pencerrig Country House outside Builth Wells, and it was in Builth that I first met my future wife Susan Jane Lewis when I was sixteen.

After Denstone I went on to Matthew Boulton College, Birmingham, where I discovered birds, booze, jazz clubs and more. After a curtailed engagement, I met Susan again. I was twenty-one, she nineteen when we married, penniless, living in a small flat in Birmingham.

After graduation I became a sales rep for a subsidiary of Unilever and we moved to a bungalow in Pencoed near Bridgend. Then I saw an ad in the *Western Mail*, owned by Thomson Regional Newspapers, and was taken on as an advertising salesman based in Swansea.

The mid-Sixties were boom years for South Wales business, and my adsales career started to boom as well. I was moved on to Industrial selling – features on factories, businesses and so on, and this too went so well that when the regional ITV station, TWW, lost its licence, I was approached to do the regional advertising sales for the new company, Harlech TV.

Nothing could have prepared me for those great years in commercial television, when it seemed that no matter what crap was transmitted the ratings went up, and up, and up, and the viewership figures made today's ratings pathetic by comparison.

Harlech TV won its licence with a board packed with glitterati like Stanley Baker, Richard Burton, and Elizabeth Taylor, and a promise to bring Culture with a capital 'C' to the deprived masses of Wales. But within weeks it was clear that those masses only felt deprived when they were force fed a diet of opera, literary discussions, and more opera. What they wanted, just like people throughout Britain, was untaxing entertainment, game shows, and plenty of sport, and it wasn't long before the culture pledges which won the franchise were quietly forgotten or relegated to dusty corners of the schedules and the ratings war returned to the normal terms of engagement.

Also on the board were great Welshmen like George Thomas, later Lord Tonypandy, and that legendary figure of broadcasting, Wynford

Vaughan Thomas, an utterly delightful man with a puckish sense of humour. The other members of the HTV board represented the three transmission areas of West, South Wales, and Welsh Language, and at one of the early meetings an English board member from Bristol turned up wearing a monocle. Wynford couldn't let this affectation go without comment and leaned across the table to warn him, 'You'll need more than one eye to keep a watch on us Welsh boys, boyo.'

My new salary was double my newspaper salary, and rising ratings made selling easier, even if we had to make video commercials for local advertisers for as little as £20 a time to go with their airtime! Soon I got another leg up the HTV promotional ladder and was asked to take over the HTV North Wales Office in Wrexham. It was a long way from the Cardiff HQ, and I was more or less my own boss, answerable only on a long telephone line to Cardiff and an even longer one to the London Office at 99 Baker Street.

Susan and I bought a fine house outside Wrexham for £3000, with the mountains above Llangollen as a backdrop. By then we had two lovely children growing up in the country, cash to spare for little luxuries, and life in North Wales, it seemed, couldn't have been much better. My HTV duties involved not only selling air time to the local market but also representing the company at eisteddfods, acting as a judge at local beauty contests, and generally putting myself about at all kinds of functions as the voice of HTV in the North.

But I was still learning about the television business and the strange people who inhabited it. Once I had sold some airtime to a Bangor furniture store and the deal involved making a video. This was in the hands of a camera crew, a producer, and his girl assistant, who were staying at the Snowdonia Park Motel bang in the middle of Snowdonia on the A5. One evening after an arduous sales meeting in Cardiff I drove up through mid-Wales to check on progress – one hell of a drive from Cardiff.

I arrived tired and dishevelled and late in the night. I asked at reception if the others had arrived. 'Oh yes', I was told, 'they asked that you go over to cabin 12 as soon as you arrived'. I knocked on the door and went in to find that the producer had been making extremely good progress – he and his pretty assistant were sitting in bed, without a stitch of clothing between them, nor even a shred of modesty. 'Sit down,' he said, 'Have a glass of wine.' So I did, and we discussed the progress of the commercial as if we were sitting across the desk back in the office.

Meanwhile the non-stop routine of parties and functions continued and I must have established myself pretty well with the business community. It was not long before I was being asked if I was 'on the square', businessmen looking at my trouser leg whilst scrunching my fingers in theirs in the most peculiar of handshakes. I was of course, being asked in a non-too-subtle way to become a freemason and I was told that I was being done a great honour – I should accept without delay, become a pillar of the business community, and use the introductions thus obtained to reap a rich harvest.

Before I could commit myself one way or the other, my life took a dramatic turn when the HTV sales director, a charming, booming man called Ron Wordley, picked me out for greater things and suggested I advance my career by going to London and joining the company's new business unit.

And so, in 1969, I was suddenly no longer a big fish in the North Wales pond, but a very small fish adrift in the ocean of the capital, looking for the 'London opportunities' I had been promised. I had no idea what these fabled opportunities were, but in the short term they appeared virtually non-existent – I had to give up my company car, sell our house in the country, and go live in digs while searching for another house as the property boom roared away, and became another armpit straphanger on the trains and tubes to 99 Baker Street every morning.

Susan and I were at desperation point, and the property market was so volatile that a house you fancied at breakfast time was £500 dearer by lunch time, and sold by the evening. For this reason I bought a small semi on an estate in Bearsted, Kent, sight unseen. It looked good enough in the advert, at £8,500 it was only a few hundred pounds more than we could afford, and almost anything was preferable to more weeks in digs.

For my first few weeks in London I thought that I had made the biggest mistake of my life and looked back with yearning to my Wrexham days. London is a very lonely place when you are new and on your own, and I relished the opportunity to tour the country selling air-time on HTV in what we called the 'Severnside test market'. Basically, though, the pleasures of selling time on commercial television, represented by bits of coloured plastic on so-called traffic boards, largely escaped me. Everyone kept screaming about the importance of 'share' as the be-all and end-all of life. Fuck the viewers and the quality of programming. If we achieved 'share' we all got mildly or seriously drunk to celebrate, whilst if we missed out we all got monstered by the Sales Director and then went out to the nearest bar to commiserate and blame each other.

One of my favourite watering holes was the Coach and Horses in the heart of London's west end at Cambridge Circus where the land-lord, Norman, revelled in his reputation as the rudest landlord in London. A minor example of his style was the afternoon when two scruffy, bearded, unwashed hippie types approached the bar and asked for two pints of beer. Norman studied them rapidly and decided that they were among the majority of the human race who were not suit-able customers for his establishment, 'Fuck off – now!' he barked. After a few expletives and some huffing and puffing about never having been spoken to like that, the hippies departed, while Norman beamed euphorically at the remaining customers, his reputation still intact.

17

It was at this time that I ended up in a serious alcoholic stupor after doing a deal with the Polish state advertising agency to run, of all things, TV commercials for canned pork.

The business was concluded by 10 a.m. and it appeared Polish custom required it to be sealed with spirit – Scottish spirit, and lots of it. I went out for a bottle of scotch, and large measures of neat whisky were downed in one on empty stomachs, accompanied by Polish toasts which sounded like 'Nostrovia'. Heads were soon spinning rapidly, and I was deputed to take our clients to lunch, after which the Poles demanded to sample the drink – and other pleasures – which Soho had to offer.

At last I managed to pour them into a taxi for the airport, and my last conscious memory was of slowly sliding down a lamp-post in Soho Square. It was there I awoke the next morning, and miraculously my pockets and the contents of my wallet were untouched. But I had never in my life felt so appalling, and was rarely ever again to plumb the alcoholic depths so comprehensively and stupidly.

After a year at HTV in London, I realised at the age of 27, business life was fast passing me by and it was time – and possibly long past time – to seek new challenges. It was then, as I read the recruitment ads in the *Evening Standard,* that I noticed one seeking applicants for the job of 'marketing services executive' in their advertising department. I applied and got the job on the strength of a dummy presentation on why a drinks manufacturer should use the *Standard* to promote his products – I guess after all the drink I had consumed for HTV, I was something of an expert in this field.

It was a good move, and proved to be a momentous one because at last it introduced me to what I soon felt was my natural home – the inky way, the boulevard of broken dreams, the historic home of newspapers and all kinds of printed media – Fleet Street.

2

JOCELYN STEVENS
The Lion that Roared

I FIRST MET Jocelyn Stevens in the autumn of 1971, when he was managing director of the *Evening Standard*, the newspaper I had just joined in a junior capacity. He was striding across Shoe Lane, wearing a long black leather coat, similar to those worn by Gestapo officers – all part of the image, I suspect. Tall, fair-haired and handsome, he looked every inch of the Rifle Brigade officer he had once been. The man had an incredible presence and, at 39, was already a well-established Fleet Street legend.

There are few men I have met in my lifetime who could instantly command the attention of an entire room without uttering a word. Jocelyn Stevens was such a man.

His aristocratic background added more mystery to a man whose grandfather, Sir Edward Hulton, on his deathbed in the 1920s, had allegedly been chiselled out of his ownership of the *Evening Standard* by Max Aitken, later Lord Beaverbrook, who from a humble Canadian background went on to own and run the most glamorous and successful British newspaper empire of its day.

Tales about Jocelyn's legendary temper are numerous – and mostly true – but like all good tales they have enjoyed a degree of embroidery in the telling over the years. Following National Service and university, Stevens bought himself *Queen* magazine with his 21st birthday inheritance, and there the legend began. One day, it is rumoured, he was walking through the editorial department and noticed the fashion editor on the phone. 'Who are you speaking to?' he mouthed. Putting her hand over the mouthpiece she whispered back, 'New York, the fashion show.' Twenty minutes later she was still on the phone when Jocelyn passed again. Once again he asked the purpose of the call. 'New York,' she replied. Jocelyn picked up a pair of scissors and disconnected her immediately, leaving her open-mouthed with the handset severed from the instrument, dangling in her hand.

Whether it is true that, around the same time, he threw a filing cabinet from a fourth-floor window into the street below, is uncertain. The point is that Jocelyn Stevens was the kind of man of whom such a story could only be too easily believed.

He brought his reputation for unpredictability with him to the *Express*. He was approached by Sir Max Aitken in the late 1960s to join Beaverbrook Newspapers and rapidly worked his way up from being Max's assistant to becoming managing director of the *Evening Standard* and then managing director of the group, leaving the bodies of former directors and senior managers littering his path to the top job. Jocelyn brought to mind Flashman of *Tom Brown's Schooldays* fame. He could detect a weakness in anyone and be on to it like a shot. He would then continue to press the poor individual's legs to the hot radiator, metaphorically speaking.

Such a victim was David Aitken, only vaguely connected to the proprietorial family. Aitken was a nice man, grey-haired and meticulous in his record-keeping. When Jocelyn was managing director of the *Evening Standard*, David Aitken was his general manager. A sliding glass partition divided his office from Jocelyn's. When Stevens wanted something he would hurl back the partition, which made a noise like a pistol shot as it reached the extent of its opening. David would leap out of his chair, a nervous tic only too obviously throbbing on the side of his face.

David kept a large tome into which he entered all the company's transactions. Every item was neatly and accurately recorded and Aitken was justifiably proud of this work of record, indeed almost of art. The partition hurtled back. 'David, bring in your book,' Jocelyn yelled. In went the victim with the precious book held tightly under his arm. 'How much did we spend on widgets last month?' he asked. David sat down and began thumbing through the pages, forward, then back. Jocelyn started drumming his fingers on the desk. David became even more nervous, making it increasingly difficult to find the elusive item as the tension grew. Minutes went by and Jocelyn suddenly leapt to his feet and shouted, 'David, pick up your book!' as he opened the window behind him. 'Throw that bloody book out of the window!' Poor David did as he was told and his precious book crashed three floors down into Shoe Lane, never to be seen again.

Staff were generally terrified of him, but I grew to have a great deal of respect and indeed affection for him. He could be stunningly charming and a great motivator. He could also be an absolute son-of-a-bitch if he felt he had been disobeyed or crossed. Yet, it wasn't always genuine temper – he sometimes deliberately orchestrated vitriol to make his point to some hapless individual who had offended.

At 9.30 every Tuesday morning we held an executive management meeting in the gloomy, airless boardroom on the third floor, which all the senior executives attended. Surrounded by his senior staff, including his industrial relations director, finance director, legal director and the general managers of the three newspapers, Jocelyn's practice was to pick on an individual and pour torrents of abuse on him. The rest of us would breathe a sigh of relief. At least for that particular meeting we had avoided being 'scapegoat of the week'. The rest of us could day-dream, half listening and admiring the John Piper signed prints of churches which lined the yellow boardroom walls in one of the few gestures towards 'culture' to be found in the Black Lubyanka, as the *Express*'s Fleet Street headquarters was popularly known. We were not very brave in Jocelyn's management meetings which on occasions, amid roars of anger, meant the end of someone's career at the *Express*. Jocelyn quite rightly expected each member of his team to know his costs and revenue figures backwards. 'I don't know' was a very dangerous answer to give in Jocelyn's presence.

Most of the focus of such meetings was on trade union affairs, for the power of 'The Brothers' was growing steadily throughout Fleet Street. During Jocelyn's 'reign' trade union matters occupied the bulk of the newspaper manager's working day. 'Consultative' type meetings with the 'chapels' (trade union sections within the newspaper industry) were considered a very important means of keeping staff informed, and hopefully reasonably sweet, especially during the dire financial straits the group passed through in the dying days of the Beaverbrook empire in the late 1970s.

One Tuesday, Jocelyn opened up on the general manager of the *Evening Standard*.

'How are the weekly meetings going with the chapels?' he asked.

'I have discontinued them,' the general manager replied.

'Why?' Jocelyn demanded.

'Oh,' came the reply, 'the chapels were just using them as a platform for negotiation. In my opinion ...' That was as far as the hapless manager got.

'Opinion!' Jocelyn yelled. 'Your opinion! You don't have opinions! I am the only one to have opinions! Fetch me this man's contract.' Exit one general manager – permanently. Jocelyn appreciated honesty and, rightly, hated not to be informed. The manager's mistake was not talking to him before discontinuing the meetings with the chapels.

Of course, the Tuesday meetings were not all gloom and doom. Jocelyn was quick-witted and had a good, if at times cruel, sense of humour. The low point of every Tuesday management meeting would be the industrial relations director's report, a dreary list of all the outstanding claims and counter-claims of every chapel in the building. The grievances ranged from the major to the mundane. At one meeting, when dealing with canteen matters, the industrial relations director mentioned that a machine-minder's assistant had found a cockroach in his mouth.

'Was it in his mouth before he entered the canteen?' asked Jocelyn, trying to keep a straight face.

Jocelyn could be extremely supportive if you told him that you had made a cock-up, but on a one-to-one basis, never in front of an audience when he would have deemed that an appropriate public whipping would be necessary for good discipline. Once, when the company was in the midst of yet another of its regular financial crises, I had to break the news to Jocelyn that I was responsible for a financial error almost sufficient to bankrupt the company.

In that particular year our corporate plan allowed for a publicity budget of £350,000, which was a considerable sum at the time – at least for Beaverbrook Newspapers. In those days the group not only had the main Fleet Street office but scaled-down models of the Black Lubyanka in Manchester and Glasgow which had been designed by the famous thirties engineer/architect Sir Owen Williams, who also designed Wembley Stadium. Beaverbrook Newspapers employed over 12,000, turned out millions of newspapers 24 hours a day for some 364 days of the year and yet barely made a profit. The £350,000 publicity budget was for the group as a whole. Unfortunately, the managing director in Manchester thought he also had £350,000 to spend and duly spent it.

I discovered the error and, since I was in charge of publicity, resigned myself to the inevitable axe and went to see Jocelyn to get it over with. He had the unnerving habit of making you stand in front of his large desk and ignored you as he continued to write in his expansive longhand on some memo he had received. Without looking up, he demanded to know what I wanted. I explained.

This misfortune was met with a guffaw of laughter from Jocelyn accompanied by the remark, 'Well, if you're going to make a cock-up make it a big one.' He was as unpredictable as that. But as a result of his attitude, our efforts were redoubled to repair the damage with an enthusiasm fuelled with relief, and we got through the crisis. The difficulty with unpredictability is that it encourages your managers to lie to you to avoid retribution, with the result that hidden problems can become catastrophes by the time they are discovered. And in the newspaper business the scale between a small problem and a disaster can be measured in millions.

Jocelyn could also be Machiavellian, to say the least, and on one occasion it took John Junor, the legendary if flawed and devious editor of the *Sunday Express*, to save me. I was then the general manager of the *Sunday Express* which in the late 1970s was selling 3.7 million copies a week. One of my responsibilities was to supervise production, which began at 11 o'clock on a Saturday morning, and finished any time after 6 o'clock on a Sunday morning when the hapless manager could go home. Printing so many copies in London and Manchester (given wastage, etc. a circulation of this size meant a print run of around four million) was a nightmare. Unreliable machinery and unreliable men were the main culprits, with an excess of alcohol playing its part in creating mayhem as the night wore on. We frequently failed to print the required number of copies.

After one particular series of 'bad runs', as they were known in the trade, Jocelyn declared that he would come in and 'sort it out'. He duly arrived one Saturday evening and stamped round the building berating everyone who crossed his path. One hapless engineer, endeavouring to repair an ancient bundle-tier, faced a torrent of abuse. A large, heavily sweating man, he was pulling desperately on a spanner as Jocelyn approached. 'Would you let this man repair your car?' he yelled at me. Had I tried such a tactic, the AUEW would have immediately downed tools, but given Jocelyn's style and presence, he got away with it. Amazingly, the run of copies was produced on time. It was the first time in many months. 'Mike Murphy will be in next week, and he'll show you how to do it as well,' was his parting shot. (Murphy was the deputy managing director at the time.)

Murphy duly arrived the following Saturday, went into his office, lay down on the settee, and asked me to wake him if anything went wrong. He then went to sleep. Lo and behold we had another good run. The following Monday, Jocelyn went to see Victor Matthews and told him that Cameron couldn't hack it, and that I would have to go, the proof being that when he, or another board member, was around, everything went smoothly. In fact, it was pure coincidence that all had gone well when Jocelyn and Murphy had been around. Even the unions told me later that good production on the nights concerned was pure chance. Junor intervened with the then chairman Victor (later Lord) Matthews, whose Trafalgar House group had bought Beaverbrook Newspapers in 1977. My job was saved.

This was far from being the only occasion when the group managing director and the editor of the *Sunday Express* crossed swords. Junor was a great hater and Jocelyn was top of his 'hate list'. Junor loathed Jocelyn with an intensity which was only matched by Jocelyn's contempt for Junor. Both men were as different as chalk and cheese. Jocelyn was the mercurial Old Etonian. Junor played the canny, devious editor who wore his humble origins often too clearly on his sleeve. Jocelyn was Machiavelli's lion to Junor's fox. But although Jocelyn would seize most people by the throat he tended to treat Junor warily – like a lion puzzling how best to get his paws on a rolled-up porcupine. Both men tended to pour poison about each other into the ears of the powerful behind the scenes rather than have a stand-up face-to-face row. At one meeting, however, Junor famously lost his temper, and told Jocelyn that his career as managing director would end with Jocelyn being carried out of the building 'in a white coat, with arm restraints'.

Jocelyn's quixotic nature came to the fore in his dealings with the unions which at times were brilliant, sometimes disastrous and always unpredictable. Part of Jocelyn liked the idea of being the 'toff' the union bosses looked up to and who had the power to dispense company largesse – and 'The Brothers' certainly knew how to ladle on the syrup when he was in one of these moods. At other times, he would rant and rave to such an extent that the chapel officials would not quite know whether he was 'doing a Jocelyn' and manufacturing a loss of temper for effect or whether, this time, he had finally gone stark staring bonkers.

At least his unpredictability kept everyone guessing. This was high-lighted to great effect during a row with the engineers' assistants who, incredibly to the outside world, had their own union chapel. The engineers' assistants were being particularly obstreperous and delaying various plant improvement schemes by a policy of 'non co-operation'.

In practice this meant that they would do as little or as much as they wanted, and refused to act on all instructions. All this was in pursuit of an absurd claim that the installation of extra ventilation trunking entitled them to an extra thirteen men, and it was vigorously resisted by the management until the day came when Jocelyn decided that enough was enough. He gave instructions to his senior managers to arrange a meeting for the following day which he would chair and at which he pledged he would 'give it to the unions straight'.

But on the day, Jocelyn went out to lunch and arrived back an hour late for the crunch meeting. He refused to have a briefing on the crisis and strode into the boardroom with his management team scuttling behind him. Far from giving it to the unions straight, he opened the meeting by asking both sides to present their case as if he were some kind of visiting judge or ombudsman.

Having listened to the prosecution and the defence, he got up from his place at the head of the table and went to sit with the chapel representatives, saying that they had presented a most convincing case. Still sitting with his bewildered new-found friends from the chapel he asked his management team – excluding himself as managing director, of course – to present their case.

Finally, having listened to both sides, he gave his considered judgement. The chapel, he decreed, had made the more convincing case and their claim should be met. The cost of the 'Stevens Settlement' was almost £250,000 at a time when the company was in serious financial difficulties. The extra men were duly hired, never to do a stroke of real work and to pick up handsome pay-outs in due course for jobs which were redundant even before they started. No wonder the chapels wanted to deal with the so-called top dogs – too often it was like stealing from a blind beggar.

Jocelyn's meetings had a habit of going on very late into the evenings, particularly when chapel matters were concerned. One evening the managers were assembled to discuss a distribution problem. Algy Goddard, Jocelyn's driver, who could have played the lead role in *Only Fools and Horses*, arrived to wait for his master – a master who on one occasion was seen to beat Algy around the head with a rolled-up newspaper from the back seat of the car as it left the building. 'Ah, Algy,' said Jocelyn, 'perhaps you would like to give us your opinion.' Algy was directed to take Jocelyn's seat at the head of the table and the management, much to their chagrin, had to listen to Jocelyn's chauffeur give his learned summary of the situation.

The day Jocelyn was fired by Victor Matthews was the end of an era. The managers were assembled in the third-floor boardroom waiting for the dreaded Tuesday meeting to begin. Unusually, Jocelyn was late. Suddenly the door burst open and, without any preliminaries, he told us he had been fired.

We couldn't believe it. For all the problems, and the grief he brought his managers, the man was a giant, warts and all. It was difficult to envisage the group without him. Word rapidly spread around the building and the union leaders came to see him, offering their condolences, their support and industrial action if necessary. To his great credit, he told them: 'The best tribute you can pay me is to go back to work, and get on with producing the newspapers.' Later that day, I helped him pack his belongings and two or three of us had a glass of brandy with him. Despite the temper, the tantrums, and the fear of the man, I found it a sad day.

Some weeks later his management colleagues gave him a farewell dinner at a hotel in Park Lane. We had all clubbed together to buy him an engraved crystal bowl. As the evening wore on, and the wine flowed, the atmosphere grew livelier. At last Jocelyn rose to speak. As he warmed to his theme – the iniquity of the management regime which had sacked him – he raised the crystal bowl above his head and started waving it around. The audience waited to see their expensive gift dashed into a thousand pieces. Mercifully, wiser counsel prevailed, the bowl was carefully removed from his fingers and Jocelyn eventually vanished into the night.

Jocelyn in due course became rector of the Royal College of Art where his brief was to modernise the organisation and make it a positive contributor to the world of design rather that some airy-fairy outlet for creative nonsense. He had to persuade the dyed-in-the wool professors to accept proper budgeting and cost control. They refused to comply, so he locked them in a room without toilets or refreshments and left them there for hours until they agreed. They eventually did, and many fled the organisation as quickly as they could, with Jocelyn's 'sacking' boot behind them.

The students were the next to be dealt with. They organised a protest, dressed themselves in skeleton-type garb and lay down like sardines, head to toe in the corridor outside his office. 'What did you do?' I asked him. 'I just strode over the top of them,' he told me. Jocelyn is a big, powerful man. The weight of those shoes on the ribcage must have been very painful indeed. I understand he continues to create positive mayhem at English Heritage, where he is now the boss. It is almost 30 years since I first met Jocelyn. He hasn't, and I doubt ever will, change. I hope he doesn't.

3

VICTOR MATTHEWS
An Unlikely Saviour

VICTOR MATTHEWS arrived as chairman of what was then
Beaverbrook Newspapers in 1978. As deputy chairman of the
construction to shipping conglomerate Trafalgar House, Matthews
had masterminded the Trafalgar House take-over of the group.
Although Sir James Goldsmith, and to a lesser extent Associated
Newspapers, had shown interest in the ailing Beaverbrook Newspapers, Trafalgar House was the only really serious contender. Had
Trafalgar not taken over, Beaverbrook Newspapers would almost
certainly have gone bankrupt.

Crippled by debt incurred by investing in new plant, and with the
once mighty titles losing circulation steadily, the Beaverbrook dynasty
was crumbling. Basically, it was beset by all the problems of a long-time
family business in which the founder and driving force, Lord Beaverbrook, had died some fourteen years earlier, and his son and heir, Sir
Max Aitken, didn't have much feel for the business.

Indeed, I remember being told by the company auditor, Peter
Heatherington, who was also the family's accountant, that a crisis hit
the company in the mid-1970s when the price of newsprint went
through the roof. He went to see Max and told him, 'We are technically trading insolvently.' Max's reply was, 'Nonsense, there's always
been plenty of money.'

A deal was struck with Trafalgar House, at a price of £13 million
for the Beaverbrook empire, which Victor was later to recover in its

entirety from the redevelopment of the old *Evening Standard* building in Shoe Lane.

Victor was a small man physically, almost squat, and with a bryl-creemed hairstyle reminiscent of the 'Fonz' of television fame – a swept-back quiff of lustrous black hair, greying stylishly at the temples. His eyes were almost black, and it was hard to know what went on behind them. He seldom smiled, and when he did there was some warmth, but not much. His business personality was best described as dour.

Until becoming chairman of Beaverbrook Newspapers at the age of 58, Victor Matthews's closest contact with the newspaper world had been as a young teenager delivering newspapers around St Paul's Road, Islington for a half a crown (12.5p) a week.

The young Victor was brought up by his mother, his father having done a runner just after the First World War. He went to a Church of England elementary school and after a spell of unemployment on leaving school, he got his first job as an office boy in the tobacco factory which produced Kensitas and Du Maurier cigarettes.

(Ironically, when a future newspaper magnate, the great twentieth-century fraudster Robert Maxwell, who was born Ludwig Hoch, decided to change his name for the first time shortly after the Second World War he called himself Robert Du Maurier after his favourite cigarettes at the time. The Maxwell came later.)

Just before war broke out, the 20-year-old Victor joined the Royal Naval Volunteer Reserve at HMS *President* on the Embankment. His first choice had been the RAF but he felt the waiting list was too long and he was impatient to get cracking. As an ordinary seaman he took part in a series of dangerous combined operations, including the raid on the Lofoten Islands and the attack on Dieppe. He admitted later that he suffered constantly from seasickness and hated his time at sea.

But by the end of the war he had the rank of able seaman and had married Joyce who was to be his wife for more than 40 years.

He joined Trollope & Colls as a trainee, got fired at some point, then slowly made his way up through the building trade, eventually developing a small building company called Bridge Walker. In the early 1960s it was bought by Nigel Broackes's Trafalgar House property and construction group, who also bought Trollope & Colls – it is said that Victor took some pleasure in sacking those who had got rid of him years before. The combination of Broackes's vision and flair and Matthews's canniness, shrewdness and management skills made for a powerful team. Through internal growth and some dramatic acquisitions such as Cementation, the international civil engineering firm, the Cunard shipping line and the Ritz Hotel, the Trafalgar Group grew and prospered. For a company which had acquired some of the famous British names, the Beaverbrook empire, ailing and near-bankrupt, provided a tempting attraction.

Like many men who started at the bottom and have made their way successfully in the world, I think that Victor Matthews was very shy as a result of his humble beginnings. But he was shrewd, and had shouldered more and more of the day-to-day running of the business, with Nigel Broackes increasingly taking a back seat although he remained prominent on the speaking, dining and conference circuit. Victor loved playing golf and, as his wealth and success grew, he developed a love of horses and the racing world. But he remained largely untouched by fame and fortune and still lived in a modest house in North London, at least by a plutocrat's standards, with his wife of 40 years.

Victor was a very private man. Broackes was never ever invited to Victor's home, nor vice versa. Indeed, I know of only one journalist who ever entered its portals (he was a financial writer who had known Matthews long before the *Express* take-over). The kitchen was modest, with a caged parrot in the corner, and Victor was perfectly at ease as his wife busied about preparing breakfast. Outside, construction workers were putting the finishing touches to part of the M25 which was about to open and which stood some 150 yards from the bottom of Victor's large but not extensive garden.

'Aren't you bothered about the possible noise?' the journalist asked.

Victor was silent for a moment and then said with a hint of pride in his voice, 'Well, you see, I got a very good price in compensation ...'

By the late 1970s, Victor was growing bored and looking for another challenge. Beaverbrook Newspapers proved irresistible. Ensconced as chairman, Victor's office was on the third floor of the black glass building overlooking Fleet Street. In previous years it had been Lord Beaverbrook's office although he rarely used it, preferring to terrorise his editors and managers by telephone from his country estate at Cherkley in east Sussex or Arlington House by London's Green Park. After the Old Man's death it remained the chairman's office and was occupied by Beaverbrook's son, Max Aitken. Victor spent a fortune using *Express* money to refurbish it. It had pale brown velvet wallpaper, and built-in fine walnut cabinets to house his TV, video and drinks cabinet. The desk and chairs would have graced the Oval Office at the White House, and in addition, there was gold-coloured metal edging to everything.

Security were called one evening to this magnificent room to find, feet up on Victor's desk, with a glass of Victor's whisky in one hand and one of his cigarettes in the other, the most disgusting, smelly tramp imaginable. The progress of the tramp was easily traced, for he had already left the distinctive, malodorous marks of his presence on a glass table in the boardroom and in the ladies' loo. Victor was at his most dour when informed of this invasion of his inner sanctum the next day.

Victor Matthews was very much an unknown quantity when he took over as Beaverbrook chairman after the fall of the house of

Beaverbrook. He clearly knew a great deal about the building industry, but what did he know about the printing world, and how much was he prepared to learn?

The early omens were not auspicious, though one of his first demands was easy enough to deal with. Victor loved a cup of tea, and wanted his own personal pot at every board meeting. The tea lady was duly instructed to start every meeting by placing his cuppa at the head of the boardroom table. At one of his early meetings, business began with the tea ritual, and there was silence until the tea lady retreated. Then the silence went on ... and on ... and on ... as Victor sat at the head of the table surrounded by all the assembled directors and gazed with furrowed brow at the ceiling. What was the problem? It was obviously greatly affecting the chairman and seemed to bode ill for the company and for all those present. Was it a take-over? Were we going bust?

At last the silence was broken with a deep and painful sigh. 'I don't know what to do,' Victor confessed and then paused. The directors waited nervously for the problem that clearly confounded their noble leader. 'I just don't know what to do about my putting ...'

Nigel Broackes, then chairman of Trafalgar House, said in his auto-biography that buying Beaverbrook Newspapers would give his deputy chairman 'something to do'. He was also unpleasant about Victor's only son Ian, stating that 'he had an O level in cabbage growing', which hurt Victor. It was, however, interesting to note the very mixed fortunes of Trafalgar House after Victor's departure when his street-wise business sense was no longer an influence on Trafalgar's business.

Victor had asked for three months of industrial peace when he took over. The engineers gave him six weeks. They were already well paid even by Fleet Street standards – £140 for a four-day week with a nominal 35 hours during the daytime and 30 hours when working on night shifts. They now demanded as much money as the highest paid printers, namely £250 a week. Victor refused. They were given an ultimatum to return to work or be dismissed. They ignored the threat for they had heard it all before.

Then they made their fatal mistake. They removed essential equipment from the foundry – the clips, bars and rings. Without these parts no printing plates could be cast and the production of newspapers immediately ground to a halt. As Matthews saw it, and his lawyers backed him up, the challenge presented by the engineers was no longer an industrial dispute. The engineers had committed theft and were guilty of criminal acts. Victor threatened to move all production to Manchester on a permanent basis and proceeded to call in the police, an action almost unheard-of in Fleet Street in those days. The industrial mood grew ugly. A fire was started in the publishing room and editorial car windscreens were smashed. Matthews had barbed wire erected around the perimeters of the *Express* building, and blockaded the front entrance like Rorke's Drift ready for the onslaught.

He asked the editor of the *Daily Express*, Derek Jameson, to write a front-page leading article headlined:

WE SHALL NOT BE MOVED

The main message of the leading article was:

Far too many within the industry have cashed in on the vulnerability of newspapers in a shrinking and highly competitive market. Fleet Street has become a jungle where anyone who dares to oppose excessive and often outrageous demands does so at the eternal risk of instant stoppage and imminent bankruptcy ... We shall not be moved.

Victor Matthews wasn't and the engineers blinked first. The new chairman's intransigence was helped by the powerful national leader of the engineers' union, Reg Birch, a man to the left of Chairman Mao, who read the riot act to the branch members. Birch always had the ultimate deterrent – the power to withdraw the all-important union cards without which members could find no work and which would have left them to the tender mercies of the police who would have been only too willing to move in on a charge of criminal damage.

Today, the terms Victor demanded seem unremarkable – no unauthorised tea breaks, no absence from work without authority, no chapel meetings during working hours, full contract working to be guaranteed, a one-third cut in staffing to be examined and the reaffirmation of 'the management's right to manage'. But at the time the settlement which Victor demanded and won was revolutionary.

The only amusing incident in this unhappy affair was the confirmation, after the settlement, of the whereabouts of the famous clips and bars. The engineers had hidden them in the boot of the managing director's car where they had remained throughout the whole of the dispute!

Of course, the deal with the engineers didn't change everything; but the print workers at the *Express* recognised that they had a new boss who was unwilling to play the game by the old rules. Victor Matthews had kicked the first brick out of the wall.

Other disputes followed. Time after time the new chairman sought recourse through the courts on a scale and with a determination never before seen in Fleet Street. He won various cases in the High Court and the Appeal Court. Using legal means to curb the powers of the print unions was one of Victor's great achievements. He was using the law even before the Thatcher government started to pass the series of trade union law reforms which were to revolutionise the industrial scene in the mid to late 1980s.

Although the main revolution in Fleet Street was carried out by Rupert Murdoch who, as we shall see, built on the pioneering work of Eddie Shah, the provincial publisher who launched his *Today* newspaper without union involvement, Victor Matthews's contribution should not be forgotten. His combination of common sense, toughness and willingness to take legal action against the unions if necessary, started to crack the union power structure and prepare the way for the Fleet Street revolution to come.

Despite the fact that Victor shared many working-class roots with the union officials, they had great difficulty in dealing with him. Victor used the fact that he was 'a working class boyo' to his advantage when he met them. He would forever regale them about his days 'on the shovel' in the building industry. This was one newspaper chairman who was not born with a silver spoon in his mouth. The unions were more accustomed to dealing with rich toffs who, they felt, they could bamboozle and rip off remorselessly.

Frequently, Victor would literally bore them out of their claims. On one such occasion the EETPU electricians, a notoriously militant lot, managed to arrange a meeting with him on a long-standing claim to maintain the computer mainframe. Apart from the horror of handing such complicated kit to people with only limited plug-changing ability, the computer mainframe contained sensitive items like the payroll records. There is an obligation of confidentiality on an employer regarding employees' personal circumstances. No employer, or employee, would want the unions getting their hands on such sensitive information.

For some years the mainframe had worked from a building outside the main complex, and was maintained by contractors. At the appointed hour the notorious EETPU management beater, Ron Cowell, and his delegation, arrived at Victor's office. As Cowell made an attempt to speak, Victor was already in full swing about the real world outside the fantasy world of Fleet Street. His monologue roamed widely, dealing at length with the problems of unemployment, what he paid electricians on building sites, the political situation and the world of work in general. Hours went by as Victor lit one cigarette after another and continued with his monologue, refusing to allow any interruptions from the union officials. Electricians' bums kept leaving their seats in an attempt to go. Victor would tell them to sit down as he hadn't finished. Three hours later he ended the meeting, and in their scramble to get out of the room, two of them got jammed shoulder to shoulder in the doorway, turning the whole thing into a farce. The electricians never did manage to put their case fully to Victor.

Victor had very straightforward views on right and wrong and on morality. He was mortified when he found out that the staid, bespectacled company secretary was having an affair with his demure bespectacled personal secretary. His company secretary was a married man, and married men did not do these things. It was said that his relationship with his trusted right-hand man was starchy, to say the least, after these revelations. As for a single woman having an affair with a married man ... Victor took a very dim view of such goings on.

Victor's one weak spot was his son Ian. There was no ill-will in Ian but, as an only child who was born, unexpectedly, when his parents were approaching middle age, Ian was the apple of his parents' eye, and had been totally spoiled as only a child of middle-aged parents can be. At a dinner party, one of the family's close friends told me that when Ian was a toddler he could do exactly as he wished, and was never admonished, no matter the nature of the childish crime.

Victor decided it would be a good idea to introduce his 18-year old to the world of newspapers and he assigned his son and heir to work with me on the production side of the business. It proved to be a nightmare. Ian was rotund and amiable with the interest and attention span of the proverbial gnat. He would be late for everything and submitted the most horrendous expenses for entertaining his toadying mates at such salubrious establishments as School Dinners, a City establishment which specialises in serving up school fare like toad-in-the hole and spotted dick with custard, served by waitresses dressed up as schoolgirls.

He once presented me with a massive claim for a week's worth of such fun. Even I, who had seen some inspired expenses claims in my time, was awestruck by his effrontery. I went to see Victor and told him I couldn't authorise it. Apart from the amount, the claim would have to be processed by the prying eyes of the cashiers. What an example that would set the staff. Victor took one look at it, and said 'I can't do anything with the little bugger either, pay him half.'

Ian also had an intense interest in dipping into the secretarial pool, seeming to feel it was the absolute right of the feudal son and heir, a modern-day version of *droit de seigneur*. With this reputation, I was astonished when my former secretary, Helen, agreed to marry Ian and moved in to live with him on his stud farm (horses were his other great passion). Helen was a delightful girl who, some four or five years previously, had tragically lost her first husband, a talented young man, at the age of 28 when he suffered an asthma attack while they were on holiday in the West Country. The marriage to Ian in fact proved successful and the couple had three children who brought their doting grandfather Victor immense pleasure in the last few years of his life.

Although Victor's talents as a newspaper proprietor were at times questionable, he had a superb business brain and a great nose for a 'deal'. When Trafalgar House bought Beaverbrook Newspapers from the Aitken family trust, Victor's real skills were shown at their best. He paid £13 million for the business and although he rather liked the idea of inheriting the former Beaverbrook newspaper empire, there is not a shadow of a doubt that the potential for property development was uppermost in his mind. Almost immediately on taking over Beaverbrook Newspapers, Victor issued instructions to integrate the *Evening Standard* into the Fleet Street building. Intense negotiations took place over many months; every detail of the move had to be planned, and massive reshuffling of everyone in the Fleet Street building undertaken to make room for the *Evening Standard* staff and equipment.

We moved the entire operation over one weekend. The last pages in hot metal form were literally trolleyed across the road, and papers were produced in Fleet Street on time. What I didn't know at the time was that a sword was hanging over my head through that intense 48 hours. Many years later, I came across a memo from Jocelyn Stevens to Victor saying that if the move went pear-shaped I was to be the sacrificial lamb.

Trafalgar House subsequently redeveloped the Shoe Lane site. Some of the printing machines, however, were lodged so deeply in the London clay that they proved impossible to move except at outrageous expense and had to be cemented over and left *in situ* where to this day they help give the Shoe Lane successor building probably the strongest foundations in London. Trafalgar sold the redeveloped building on for £13 million, the sum it had paid for the entire Beaverbrook empire.

Game, set and match to Victor.

4

VICTOR'S RISING STAR

THE COMBINATION of tougher industrial discipline, begun with the victory against the engineers six weeks after Matthews took over the helm at Beaverbrook Newspapers, and stricter financial controls introduced by the new owners, began to have their effect on the bottom line. The group started to show signs of moving from loss into profit. At this stage, in February 1978, Matthews made the symbolic gesture of renaming the group Express Newspapers. The Beaverbrook era was truly over.

At the same time Matthews was looking for ways of developing the potential of the newspaper group he had taken over in such rushed and unusual circumstances. He was moved by a belief that he would express to anyone when he had the chance. 'Fleet Street is not overmanned,' he would say. 'It is underworked.' He knew that at least for the foreseeable future, there was no way any Fleet Street management could challenge the then existing structure of union power. However, he decided that the one thing he could achieve was to make the fullest possible use of existing facilities and manpower in London and Manchester – especially at the Manchester office where a considerable amount of plant and machinery lay idle for large parts of the day.

Various ideas were thrown around – a new evening paper, a business paper and even a new Sunday paper were all suggested in their time. Research was carried out, small working parties were formed and some dummy layouts for the proposed new newspapers were drawn up.

Yet the big decision came out of the blue and involved very little research or preparation.

Returning with Jocelyn from an NPA meeting one day, Victor remarked that when industrial action in Bouverie Street kept *The Sun* off the streets, the *Daily Express* picked up sales. But when *The Sun* went on sale again, the extra *Daily Express* sales evaporated. This led Victor to conclude that what Express Newspapers needed was a 'popular' newspaper to challenge *The Sun* and the *Daily Mirror* in their territory, using Express Newspapers' under-employed plant and machinery.

Thus was the *Daily Star* born – with a gestation period of only twelve weeks. Launched on 2 November 1978 in Manchester, the *Daily Star* for the main part used existing Express staff. The twelve-strong London bureau was staffed by *Express* journalists.

The first editor of the *Daily Star* was Peter Grimsditch, usually known as Grimbles. He was very much the choice of Derek Jameson, then editor of the *Daily Express,* who also became editor-in-chief with overall responsibility for the *Daily Star.* Jameson had a high regard for Grimsditch. They had worked together on the *Sunday Mirror.* Says Jameson:

> He looked like a manic Steve MacQueen and had immense drive and a great capacity for work. Emotional, noisy, reckless – but still superb at his job. Just the man to edit a new, down-market tabloid.

'What's he done ... this Grimm-er-um ...?' Matthews wanted to know. Like many others, he could never quite get the hang of Grimsditch's name. Grimsditch's claim to the editor's chair was none too promising. His top job to date had been as deputy editor of the defunct weekly

Reveille. Grimsditch, long-time Murdoch employee, was the man, his ex-wife used to say, 'who put the tits in *Reveille*'. (Circulation went up for the first time in eleven years.) However, Victor and Jocelyn brightened considerably when Jameson told them that Grimsditch was a classical Greek scholar with an honours degree from Oxford. They agreed to give him the job.

Phil Rostron was one of the first journalists to work on the *Daily Star* since the beginning and served under every editor employed at various stages to man the tiller of what became a very troubled ship. Of Grimsditch he says:

> Peter Grimsditch was one of the cleverest men I ever worked for. He was a slight, bespectacled chap with a shock of fair hair and piercing blue eyes. He had a distinctly sunny nature and could often be heard guffawing his way through conferences and during discussions with executives on the editorial floor.

Grimsditch believed that while a newspaper should educate and inform it should never lack 'fun value', one of his favourite sayings being, 'What is life for if it isn't for a laugh?'

Finding a 'splash' for the front cover on launch day was nigh impossible. Finally, Grimsditch settled on a model whose career had been threatened by a fall from her flat in a high-rise block. Hence the new *Daily Star*, the first national newspaper to be launched for 75 years, greeted the world with the news of a 'Model's Mystery Plunge'. Actually, the girl involved had been an 'aspiring' model and she had taken a tumble no more than three feet from the ground floor, so she hardly sustained serious injuries. But Grimsditch had started as he meant to go on by never letting the facts stand in the way of a good story.

Grimsditch's search for 'fun' became increasingly quirky. Once, having seen a picture of a flamingo standing on one leg, he decided that it would be 'fun' to run a series of photographs with animals or humans standing flamingo-style. Sports stars and building labourers were, for a time, prepared to join in the joke but it quickly became tedious and was quietly dropped.

His recruitment methods for news staff were unique and not one you will find in a Total Quality Management manual. He didn't believe in interviewing the job applicant from behind his desk when they turned up at the Manchester office's Black Lubyanka. After having checked the applicant's credentials beforehand he would line the person up in the news room, surrounded by his key staff, saying, 'I'm the editor, these are my executives and the way we will conduct this interview is that I will jump on to this desk, sing the first line of a song and whether or not we employ you will depend upon your perform-ance in completing the song.'

Having jumped on to the 'stage' from a standing position (Grims-ditch was a past master at this party trick), he would begin 'I left my heart in San Francisco ...' and the job applicant would have to attempt to leap on to the desk from a standing position, scramble up and continue the song. Sufficient applause from the assembled executives would guarantee the production of a contract.

For the journalists, the *Daily Star* under Grimsditch was full of schoolboy fun and laughter – the sort of enthusiasm which a new baby brings with all those great hopes for the future.

'Come on and reach for a *Star* – at 6d its gotta be Britain's best buy', screamed the television ads.

But it wasn't to last.

At first, Derek Jameson had been glowing in his tributes to his protégé, Grimsditch, who he claimed 'had put the *Star* together from scratch, grafting up to sixteen hours a day to make the paper succeed and secure the staff's jobs.' It was launched with the smallest staff of any national newspaper, little money to spend and massive production problems.'

But Jameson was the editor-in-chief, which is never a satisfactory appointment for it inevitably creates tension between the incumbent and the editor of the newspaper who technically 'reports' to the editor-in-chief. It was hardly surprising that an uneasy relationship soon developed between Jameson and Grimsditch, with the latter increasingly deliberately keeping Jameson out of the information 'loop'. This created growing disagreements between Grimsditch and the management and developed into a series of slanging matches, whereupon Victor Matthews and Jocelyn Stevens exercised the Jameson-as-editor option. Grimsditch was fired in March 1980 for failing to maintain proper relations with Jameson.

Jameson was instructed to go to Manchester, deliver the chop personally and take over the *Daily Star*.

Of the firing, Grimsditch said:

What the hell does a man have to do to keep his job? I'd given them a newspaper that was selling. By the time they sacked me, the circulation had gone up to 1.2 million. I'd given them a newspaper from scratch that was selling 1.2 million copies per day ... So I left them their car, playing Beethoven's Seventh, with the engine running, sunroof open, on Fleet Street, outside the black glass building.

Jameson was, for a time, left running two papers – 'We get two editors for the price of one,' Victor told Jocelyn jocularly. But Jameson accepted the joint role with little enthusiasm. He soon became known in Manchester as the 'editor in absentia', spending more and more time building up his broadcasting career. No newspaper can last long without a captain on the bridge and Jameson was replaced by Lloyd Turner, a gruff Australian who had made his name and crucified his liver as night editor of the *Daily Express*.

'Gather round,' Turner barked as he made his first entrance before embarking on revealing his blueprint for the success of the newspaper. He believed that the way forward was for the *Star* to adopt the great traditions of British journalism. 'I passionately believe,' Turner intoned gravely, 'in campaigns in defence of the little man, the correction of injustice, the breaking down of red tape ...' All this was to be achieved without losing sight of the importance of sport and entertainment. 'We are the sword that strikes the mighty ...'

According to Rostron, the 'overview' of his third editor in three years sounded as though it had come from a primer in a first-year class in journalism. Maybe it was corny, but the journalists liked it and, combined with the newspaper bingo craze in which the *Star* led the way, the circulation rose to 1.7 million. Turner was naturally elated. 'Gather round' was the regular order of the day as he imparted the latest weekly sales figures. 'There is still much to do, the battle has only commenced ...'

The more successful the paper grew, the more paranoid Turner became about secrecy. His three-day-long think tanks, commonly known as 'drink tanks', were held in a sumptuous hotel and became famous for Turner's attempts to sniff out any suspected mole. Each of the executives was presented with an itinerary and the points for discussion amounting to a hundred or more pages of close type. A single word or phrase was changed in the set which each executive received to satisfy Turner's belief that a word-for-word repetition of one of the ideas would identify the 'mole' in his team. This preposterous situation, which displayed a lack of trust on the editor's part, was deeply resented by the senior staff.

It was said that you could tell Turner was lying because you could see his lips move. He drank champagne heavily, believing it was non-alcoholic, and it was when he was in his stupors that he would promise his staff cars, bonuses, etc. without any prior discussion with the management who were driven crackers trying to unravel the mess. The axe was finally to fall on Lloyd Turner, largely due to his landing the group in the disastrous Jeffrey Archer libel trial.

Victor's *Daily Star* was a bold idea. Unfortunately, by the time he had it up-and-running, his brave venture had led to an additional 1000 staff being taken on with the entire staff in the group being paid 'Star Money'. So much for being underworked. The birth of the *Star* created the biggest gravy train of all time for the unions. There was no group of employees who failed to dip their bread in the rich gravy. Even managers were paid extra 'Star Money' right up to all but the most senior level.

And yet ... the *Daily Star* was an imaginative attempt by a man who realised that something had to be done about the overweening and disastrous power of the unions and had a good stab at doing it. Unfortunately, the climate was just not right when Victor set out to slay the union dragon. The dramatic changes which finally led to the breaking of the power of the print unions and the transformation of Fleet Street still lay almost a decade ahead of the day he launched his newspaper. The paper will never be remembered for the brilliance of its editors. It will always be Victor's *Daily Star.*

Victor was anxious to be recognised as a publisher and a man of substance in his own right. He was an ardent Thatcherite and often spoke to 'Margaret'. He would proffer his political views at some length in a somewhat naive and black-and-white way. Once his mind was made up, his views were not negotiable; after all, why confuse your views with the facts?

His straightforwardness could embarrass the 'sophisticated'. At one lunch in the fifth-floor dining room, he entertained Sir Geoffrey Howe, then Foreign Secretary. Victor had invested a tidy sum in a golf and luxury villa complex at Sotogrande in southern Spain, just across from the border of Gibraltar where border restrictions made transfer between the British colony and Spain very difficult. To reach Sotogrande Victor had to fly to Marbella and make the long journey along the coast to his destination. All during the lunch with Howe, Victor bent the Foreign Secretary's ear without pause. He laid his case on with a trowel. His years 'on the shovel' had taught him directness, not subtlety, in getting his way. Shortly afterwards a border agreement between Gibraltar and Spain was reached and Victor was able to fly directly to Gibraltar. Of course, the agreement had nothing to do with Victor. The negotiations had been going on for years and were reaching a conclusion anyway. But Victor liked to think that he had helped change the course of history at least in a small way.

Although he had no real 'feel' for newspapers, this lack did not prevent his having views about how his newspapers should look, and he would proffer his suggestions to whoever happened to be editor of the *Daily Express* or *Daily Star* (he tended to keep off Junor's patch on the *Sunday Express*). This would lead to some tense confrontations especially during the three years (1982–5) when Sir Larry Lamb sat in the *Daily Express* editor's chair. He and Larry Lamb were both working-class boys who had done well. Both, Victor from London, Larry from Yorkshire, were as stubborn as mules. But despite their occasional 'differences of opinion' both men retained a warm, if wary, respect for each other.

Despite the gradual turn-around in the fortunes of Express News-papers, the newspaper group was regarded as a continual thorn in the side of Trafalgar House – the profligacy of national newspapers in those days being somewhat prejudicial to a building company run on spartan lines. As a result of ever growing conflicts, and with the agreement of Trafalgar House, Victor formed a company called Fleet Holdings in 1982, a decision which helped lead to Jocelyn's dismissal. Fleet Holdings brought together two businesses, Express Newspapers and Morgan Grampian, the magazine group also owned by Trafalgar and which was called 'The Jewel in the Crown' by Victor, much to the chagrin of everyone at the *Express*.

Fleet Holdings was one of the first of the successful demergers accepted by the Stock Exchange. It made Trafalgar House happier for they had never become reconciled to Fleet Street salary levels and the general atmosphere of the national newspaper business. The pitiful pay rates in the construction business meant that, for example, the *Express* finance director was paid almost double that of the head bean-counter at Trafalgar House, until Victor forced a pay cut on the hapless *Express* man. 'It's either that or you go,' said Victor, never an emotional man.

Towards the end of its few short years of independence, Fleet Holdings had its head office in the former Rank Films headquarters in South Street, Mayfair. This was a magnificent mansion with a tarty Cecil B. deMille type staircase, sweeping down on to a black and white marble entrance hall with sumptuous offices and full catering on call. All that was missing were the casting couches of yesteryear. It suited Ian Irvine, an accountant who had become Victor's chief executive, and his four or five staff who rattled round the building like peas in a drum. There was a spare Rolls-Royce in the mews garage in case either Victor's Rolls or Irvine's Bentley happened to break down – a world of extravagance miles away from the shabby offices in Fleet Street perched on top of one of the last genuine factories in London.

When Fleet Holdings was formed it was listed immediately on the Stock Exchange at 20p and sank rapidly to 15p. Victor gave share options to all senior managers, most of whom felt that they had been handed a pig in a poke. But within two years David Stevens's United Newspapers had made an aggressive bid for Fleet Holdings and, after a fearsome corporate battle, Fleet Holdings fell to the predator. I was on holiday when the bid came to a conclusion: I received a call from the *Express* managing director Mike Murphy. 'They've got us, cock,' he said.

Nervousness and insecurity swept over me. 'The good news is they've paid £3.65 a share.' Insecurity swept from me. I was lucky enough to hold 80,000 share options and they had to be realised. When the cheque arrived at my home my wife and I put it on the kitchen table and stared at it for a long time. It was a set of gold teeth for many people and nobody more so than Victor who pocketed about £11 million and rapidly disappeared to Jersey to live.

Victor's parting words, pockets bulging, at his farewell dinner at South Street were, 'You'll all be OK with David Stevens.'

Little did he know.

5

LORD STEVENS
The City Comes to Fleet Street

I FIRST MET Lord – then just plain David – Stevens for the first time as my boss in 1985 in his sumptuous office in the City of London in a square just off Liverpool Street. This was the headquarters of MIM, the pension fund manager, which he had built up from small beginnings to become a power in the financial world of the Square Mile by the 1980s. He was also a non-executive chairman or director of a number of other businesses both in the UK and abroad. Above all, by the early 1980s he had become the executive chairman of United Newspapers and chaired the bulk of the subsidiary companies in the group which included prestige titles such as the *Yorkshire Post*.

Very much a hands-on man, David Stevens was small in stature (something he frequently joked about in a slightly defensive sort of way, which perhaps revealed a certain 'chip on the shoulder' aspect to his character). He was a dapper man who always dressed in beautiful hand-made suits and with shoes polished to a gleam by his Filipino manservant. Swept back iron-grey hair topped an impish face. His eyes were fascinating but extremely disconcerting: very pale grey framed by fairly strong glasses.

In the City of London there are more crooks to the square yard than there are in Parkhurst. Many of them are keystones in their own communities and never get caught. For this lot to have christened Stevens 'slippery' must have been a begrudgingly bestowed compliment on a man they recognised as faster and quicker at the money-making game than they were. Stevens was, quite properly, very proud of the fact that his grandfather had been a railway signalman, and money had been very tight. His father amassed a fortune by inventing Britain's first portable hearing aid. He was a quiet man who gave large sums to charitable causes; he sent young David to Stowe public school from where he went to Cambridge where he graduated with honours in economics and a blue for golf.

His National Service was spent as a second lieutenant in the army in Hong Kong. I remember him telling me about a boxing match he had won on board a troopship bound for Hong Kong. Stevens, who in those days tipped the scales at around eight stone and was 5ft 4in tall, knocked out a stoker to win the trophy. He was long puzzled about his victory, because apart from knowing hardly anything about boxing and being terrified and half-blind without his glasses as he entered the ring on the afterdeck of the ship, he barely remembered landing the first round knock-out blow. Later, it became clear when his orderly, who happened to be the China Fleet heavyweight champion, confessed to having threatened to beat the living daylights out of Stevens's hard-fisted navy opponent if the man didn't take a dive in the first round.

This was the man who took over the chairmanship from the very different Victor Matthews after the successful United Newspaper's take-over bid for Fleet Holdings. With David Stevens you were never quite sure which way he was going to jump even when you had known him a long time. You could get your approach to a subject badly wrong, whereupon he could not only be unpleasant but extremely nasty, although he rarely was with me. Once he had his knife out for someone, his days were numbered. 'So and so is an old lag,' he would say to me about some hapless soul who had offended him. 'Get rid of him!' I usually managed to stave off the inevitable execution day for months, but in the end David Stevens would have his way.

Occasionally execution would be instant. On one of his first tours of the Black Lubyanka in Fleet Street following the United Newspapers take-over, I was escorting him around the building. At one stage we descended into the bowels of the earth to the machine room, where the newspapers were printed throughout the night. It was a dark, hot area, shaking with the roar of the mighty printing machines and always reminded me of the engine room of a ship. This area was a hotbed of union activity and occupied by denizens of the night who rarely made an appearance in daylight.

As I explained the printing process to Stevens, I was suddenly aware of a figure approaching our party from our rear, steering an unsteady course towards us. It was Reg Kibble, machine-room manager for years and the scourge of managers and chapels alike, a king in his own gloomy kingdom, and a well-reputed drunk tolerated by previous managements for his knowledge and for the fear he struck into the hearts of all when under the weather. Reg was so well recognised by the bucolic establishment of Fleet Street that he had his own permanent chair at the bar of the City Golf Club. The latter was a local watering hole which had nothing to do with golf, although when it opened it had an electronic golf range which was broken in its first week. Reg's tipple at his 'golf club' was a large Gordon's gin and tonic with no ice or lemon which he consumed by the bucketful – at least a bottle a day.

In my heart I was fond of the old boy and was praying that he would veer past us and disappear into the machine minders' 'den'. Reg would have none of it. Swaying from side to side, he came up to Stevens. A thick fog of alcoholic fumes sufficient to asphyxiate even hardened drinkers crossed the floor. 'Chairman,' he slurred. 'I'm Reg Kibble, your machine-room manager. If there's anything I can do for you ...' – all this in words so indecipherable it was hard even for me to understand Kibble. Stevens turned to me and barked, 'This man is drunk – sack him!' And that was the end of a machine-room manager of thirty years' service. Stevens had started as he meant to go on.

Word of Kibble's departure swept the building like wildfire. A feared old soldier had been executed. 'Killer' Stevens's reputation was established instantly as that of a hard man who would not tolerate old Fleet Street activities under any circumstances, particularly drinking on duty. Drink-hardened journos ordered orange juice at lunches when he was present, an act of self denial which rather amused him. After 6 p.m., however, his gin and tonics would have done due credit to any poured in the Street of Shame.

Our next port of call that evening was the composing room, another area where managers trod carefully. This was the area where the pages were assembled prior to printing. Stevens had heard about work rotas and suspected scams of the highest magnitude. 'Show me your rotas,' he said to Gordon Ribbons, a first-class manager, who was coping well in extremely stressful conditions. Ribbons approached with rota in hand. As he got close to Stevens, the new chairman roared, 'This man has been drinking!'

The rota was immediately forgotten as I fought for Ribbons's job. I explained that Gordon was a most abstemious man, who, after a hot first four hours in the composing room enjoyed no more than a pint of beer with his supper at the Punch Tavern over the road. 'Are you sure?' Stevens demanded. 'I can assure you, chairman,' I replied, 'there is no better manager than Gordon.' As I said this I was struck with a terrible fear. If Stevens's witchhunt for alcohol fumes continued throughout our tour, I would be lucky to have a single senior manager, journalist or any other employee left at the end of the evening. Fortunately for me, and everyone else on duty that night, he decided to end his visit abruptly as he had to go off to a dinner engagement.

David Stevens originally became involved in newspapers with the small, somewhat insignificant provincial newspaper group, United Newspapers, in the early 1980s. Lord 'Bill' Barnetson was then chairman of United Newspapers and its principal asset was the *Yorkshire Post*. Barnetson was wise enough to recognise that the company needed financial advice if it was going to make progress, and David Stevens had been brought to his notice as the company's fund manager. He invited the young Stevens, then in his mid-thirties, to join the board. The deputy chairman was Gordon Linacre – later Sir Gordon – who had been a much decorated wartime bomber pilot and former editor of the *Yorkshire Post*, whose great claim to fame was that he had discovered the famous *Daily Express* columnist, Jean Rook, when he hired her as a young reporter for the *Yorkshire Post* years previously.

Lord Barnetson died suddenly at the age of 60 and the chairman's job became vacant. Gordon Linacre was the automatic successor, but after much heart-searching he stepped aside to allow David Stevens to take the chair. From then on, United Newspapers was on its way. Stevens was a master of the wheeling-dealing tactics of the City. From a turnover of £23 million in the early 1980s, the company grew, principally by acquisition, to reach a turnover of £950 million by the mid-1990s with profits of around £140 million and some 12,000 people in its employ around the world, principally in the UK, USA and South-east Asia.

After acquiring Express Newspapers in 1985, all managers of any status were sent for and interviewed by Stevens and Linacre. Stevens was convinced that anybody who had had anything to do with Fleet Street was bound to be drunken and useless. He had decided that he, personally, would decide whether an individual was worth continuing to be employed. Advanced notice of these interviews filled the Express senior management with foreboding. We had heard of one famous sacking at MIM when Stevens had sent for a director, given him a huge bollocking, refused to listen to anything the man had to say, and then shown him the door. Ten minutes later the man who should rightly have been dismissed arrived for his appointment. Stevens was not a man to mess with. Anyway, I passed the 'Stevens Test'.

At the point of take-over, the incumbent managing director was Mike Murphy, a man famous for his love of whisky and race horses. Some years previously he had suffered a heart attack in his forties under the demanding regime of Jocelyn Stevens whom he served as deputy for some years. As the United Newspapers' take-over for Fleet Holdings was in its final process of completion, Mike asked me to attend a dinner in the fifth-floor dining room of the Black Lubyanka for the new chairman-to-be and his wife. There were to be four of us: David and Mrs Stevens, Mike and myself. At the appointed hour a huge brown Rolls-Royce pulled up, the chauffeur got out and opened the car door. Mike and I accompanied the new chairman and his wife to dinner. Amid a barrage of questions from Stevens I got a taste of what was to come. Obviously my answer to one of his queries was inadequate and Stevens responded sharply. His delightful second wife Melissa, who was a sweetheart and was to die in a tragic accident some years later, sensed my discomfort, leant across the table and addressed me in her rich, central European accent: 'Take no notice of him, He's always like that.'

Life with David Stevens, a partnership of over ten years, was on its way.

A couple of weeks later, with the deal complete and the deeds to Express Newspapers firmly lodged in his back pocket, Stevens arrived to take control. Mike Murphy went quickly, and Stevens installed a new managing director, Roger Boase, who had been headhunted from the Mirror Group and had the active backing of Gordon Linacre,

Stevens's deputy, whose views on newspaper matters Stevens bowed to, particularly in the early months.

Nobody realised that although Boase was called 'managing director' at the Mirror Group, he was actually the advertisement director, and he hadn't a clue how to run a business. Boase was a small, balding man with the smile of a weasel. One of his first executive decisions was to bring his secretary to the Express with him, announcing that she was his 'executive assistant'. He instructed that she be paid a vast salary, given a car, and be made a member of the senior management pension fund whose membership was made up of only the directors of the company and some very senior non-board managers. It became apparent very quickly that her duties were probably of a Ugandan nature as far as Boase was concerned.

I was appointed Boase's deputy and, as a result, was in pole position to view the shenanigans in the inner sanctum. What I didn't appreciate or expect was the continual onslaught from Boase's wife who would phone me in a distraught state to ask me, 'Who is he screwing now?'

She also told me that Boase had maintained a previous mistress in a house just down the road from the marital home. When the inevitable confrontation came between wife and mistress, it took place at the mistress's home. Boase's wife marched in and was 'gobsmacked', she said, to find it decorated and furnished exactly like the marital home. Presumably, this was to ensure that Boase didn't get lost or confused.

I found myself in a difficult position. I had my boss's neurotic and unstable wife on the phone yelling about her husband's shortcomings. It got worse. Terry Esterbrook, the man who was Boase's chauffeur and in due course mine, often drove Boase's wife around for shopping, etc. He used to be regaled by her with the same torrent of abuse about her husband to which I was regularly and unwillingly subjected.

Terry was a good-looking lad and, one night after he had driven her back to the family home, she asked him if he found her attractive and invited him to come in and 'do the business' with her to 'get her own back' on her wayward husband. Poor Terry was terrified and drove off as fast as he could, feeling only too grateful to have had such a narrow escape.

Roger Boase did not last long at the *Express* although it was his managerial incompetence rather than his sexual exploits which brought about his downfall. I was forced to play the role of Brutus and stitch him up as soon as possible in order to ensure the survival of the company. Trading profits/losses were critical. Newspapers are a high cash-flow business, both in and out. Under Boase there was more 'out' than 'in'. Containing costs under the Boase regime was like trying to hold water in a colander.

One financial discipline which the Express Group had developed to a fine art over the years was the close scrutiny of our weekly trading sheets which kept directors informed of the financial state of the company in considerable detail. As a result of these sheets it was frequently necessary to take quick corrective action to stem any cash haemorrhaging which might threaten to push the ship on to the rocks. The trading sheets, therefore, played a critical role in ensuring the company's continuing progress.

When Boase first arrived on the scene in his white company-owned XJ6 Jaguar, complete with white plastic 'spoilers', and an insistence on fresh flowers in his office every day, I took in the week's trading sheets for him to review. He brushed them aside with his hand saying, 'I'm not interested in all that.' He went on to elaborate. 'The answer lies in marketing. We will only hold marketing meetings from now on, and we will produce colour every day in the *Daily Star*.'

Even in the mid-1980s newspapers were all produced in black and white, unlike today when all printing is done with the colour pages being printed 'on the run' on the newspaper printing presses. In those days the only way to include colour in a newspaper was to organise 'pre-print' colour by arranging for colour pages to be printed ahead of the day of publication at a specialist print plant on special paper. The colour reels were specially printed in Liverpool then trucked down to London. There they were put on the press and printed with the black-and-white text around the colour 'patches' which were usually advertisements.

The whole process was hugely expensive, and very difficult to produce effectively. Paper wastage levels were phenomenal. Virtually all the staff received 'colour' money, although most of them had nothing to do with the process, and the papers were usually late in reaching the shops, thus missing all the casual sale to people going early to work. They also invariably missed the home delivery runs because, by the time the papers got to the shops, the delivery boys and girls had long gone to school.

This was the haphazard 'pre-print colour' marketing strategy on which Boase planned to build up the *Daily Star*'s circulation. He also insisted that we print all our titles on heavier-weight paper. There was nothing intrinsically wrong with this idea since the better the newsprint, the better the quality of the reproduction. But the decision was hugely expensive and the financial losses soon started mounting. By the time Stevens had 'rumbled' Boase, they were to prove staggering.

Unfortunately, Stevens was new to Fleet Street, and although few could read a bottom line better, he was reluctant to intervene in the face of the newly appointed and headhunted newspaper management 'expert'. He was insufficiently confident of the *ancien régime* at the *Express* at that stage to pay much attention to us. The situation was not helped by Boase's arrogance towards Stevens. He took the line, 'I'm your chief executive and I know what I'm doing'. This is never a good stance to take with any chairman, especially someone like Stevens, and particularly if, as in Boase's case, he didn't know what he was doing. Stevens, with some prompting from the older, experienced *Express* management hands finally realised that Boase was leading us all a merry dance and he was summarily fired before the damage was beyond recovery. As a result, I received a phone call at home in the late summer of 1986 from Stevens asking me to become managing director.

Suddenly my life on a Sunday morning changed dramatically. My telephone would ring from the Stevens home where he had spread all the financial trading sheets of the *Express* on his sitting-room floor and he would question me about variances against the budgets. The production of paper from our accounts department was staggering. Over 10,000 items per month were charged to bought ledger. More than 500 expense sheets a week had to be dealt with, many of which were stunning works of creative imagination. The costs of dozens of departments and many subsidiary companies were provided in detail. Stevens would pick off individual items and expect me to have the answer there and then to them all.

After a few months in the job, when he began to understand more about the business and his confidence grew, these inquisitions lessened and in due course were replaced by more sociable meetings in his office. In addition, he conducted properly structured board meetings for the first time in the company's history, with each director reporting on his sphere of influence and Stevens picking them off like ducks in a shooting gallery when they couldn't answer his question or tried to fudge it. At such meetings, he would come in and quickly establish his dominance. One of my colleagues likened the performance to a lion coming into a cage and peeing in every corner just to show everyone who was boss.

Stevens could be very unpleasant to and about individuals on the *Express* board, and quickly let his displeasure be known by a word or a look. A David Stevens tantrum was not a pretty sight to behold and could prove devastating for the individual concerned. Such an incident would form his opinion about the victim of his wrath for a long time to come. Once he had made up his mind, their fate was sealed.

At the same time his sense of humour was dry and could be very amusing at times. As part of the plans for our exodus from Fleet Street, a new headquarters building had to be constructed and a site was purchased on the Thames at the southern end of Blackfriars Bridge. It was a costly project involving many meetings with builders, financiers, architects, etc. Our chosen partner was Sir Robert McAlpine. A large meeting took place at MIM's HQ in the City. Around the table were Lord (Edwin) McAlpine backed by his capable son David, Stevens, myself, plus a myriad of city types looking for their percentage – lawyers, accountants, bankers, the sort of City people who create nothing, but live well off the creative ideas of others.

The meeting rumbled on with each of the blue suits fighting for their say. I could see Stevens getting bored with the cacophony of voices. He tapped the table for silence, and turned to Lord McAlpine. Everyone waited for him to make some succinct point. 'Will the building site be covered with huts full of men drinking tea?' he enquired. The City suits didn't know what to make of it and silence reigned. I fell about laughing and as soon as Lord McAlpine gave a polite laugh the suits followed in chorus.

Stevens had little love for creative people whom he saw as profligate spenders without any bottom line responsibility. On one occasion, as the new building took shape, Fitzroy Robinson, the architects, were showing Stevens progress on site complete with hard hats, boots, etc. They very much looked the part. The outside cladding of the building was to be a pale grey marble, with polished steel dividers between the panels. Stevens wanted a smooth finish to both marble and steel, which he felt would stay cleaner under the onslaught of central London's atmosphere. (He is obsessive about cleanliness.) The architect was arguing fiercely that it would be more aesthetically pleasing to have some rough surface patches, and burnished as opposed to polished steel. I could hear the time bomb clock start to tick in Stevens's head. I recognised the danger signs but the architect didn't.

'Whose bloody building is it?' he demanded of the by now quivering architect, 'and who's the chairman?' 'You are of course,' came the reply. 'Well it's going to be bloody well smooth then, isn't it?' Stevens snapped.

Stevens is a proud, and rather vain, man; and when it came to naming the building the obvious choice to his mind was 'Ludgate House'. After all, David Stevens had recently become Lord Stevens of Ludgate, which was a source of constant pride to him. It was also decided, prompted by the ever obsequious *Sunday Express* editor, John Junor, that there should be a bust of his lordship in the front hall. 'After all,' oiled Junor, 'Beaverbrook had one in the foyer of the Fleet Street building.' The bust of Lord Stevens was duly created. Lord Beaverbrook's bust was modest in size and was by Epstein. Stevens's bust was enormous, and was plonked prominently on a marble plinth in the foyer of the new building with the whole effect being almost life-size: a magnificent finishing touch to a magnificent building!

Almost immediately some wag went out and bought a large pair of plastic feet with bright red toenails which were placed at the bottom of the plinth. The effect was hilarious, giving staff arriving for work a great chuckle. (This Stevens statue with its grandiose 'Stalin' touch was one of the first items to go when Lord Hollick took charge in 1997 and Stevens became non-executive.)

Lord Stevens's office at Ludgate House was magnificent. It occupied the entire length of the ninth floor overlooking the Thames with a backdrop of St Paul's Cathedral and the City of London skyline. Butler service was always on hand, and tea or coffee delivered in porcelain cups on a silver tray. The entire management of the company, together with their desks and other furniture, could have fitted into the chairman's office with room to spare. The fittings were superb and the furniture was very fine indeed. Concealed lighting and dozens of yards of electrically operated curtains created the effect of the best suite at a fine hotel. A private lavatory and shower suite were installed, hidden behind a concealed door. This was an essential fitment. Stevens was much occupied with health concerns, and obsessed with his bowel movements which occurred at particular times of the day brought on by his large daily plateful of 'All Bran'. We would be in the middle of a discussion when he would get up from his desk and say, 'Got to go for a crap', and disappear rapidly behind the hidden door.

Whereas the insecure, unsmiling suits – the management – lived on the sixth floor, from there downwards Express Newspapers was housed in somewhat more spartan but nevertheless pleasant conditions. The bean-counters didn't believe in working any longer than they had to, though they made much song and dance about getting to work before dawn had a chance to crack. The idea was to impress Stevens, who was rumoured to check the read-outs from their electronic identity tags. Each time staff went in or out of the building, a microchip in grey plastic identity cards, which mini-executives wore ostentatiously on chains around their necks, transmitted a signal to register time and date of entry and exit, including, of course, lunchtime. I don't believe that Stevens wasted his time on the comings and goings of these people, most of whom he wasn't aware existed. Staff used the early starts as what they saw as brownie point time, to enjoy cups of coffee, read newspapers at their leisure and probably treat themselves to the added bonus of free telephone calls to relatives living in inconvenient time zones such as Australia or New Zealand.

Once, he made one of the strangest remarks I have ever heard a senior executive put to an employee. Jim Anderson, our managing editor, was in the chairman's office for a meeting. Jim was a big man, maybe 6ft 3in and 16 stone. Stevens walked around Anderson's chair and said to him, 'Is it true that big men have small pee-pees?' I don't recall Anderson's reply.

David Stevens was, I believe, sadly wronged by City opinion over his relationship with Robert Maxwell. Following Maxwell's death, and as the scandal unfolded, the City rats ran for cover. Erstwhile 'friends' of Maxwell, who had gone through all manner of humiliations to curry favour with the monster at his peak, suddenly claimed that they had in reality little to do with Maxwell and 'didn't really know him'.

When David Stevens heard of Maxwell's death he said how sorry he was because he had liked him, and had regarded Maxwell as a friend. It is easy, with the benefit of hindsight, for others to put the boot in. I never worked for Maxwell, but he was always charming to me in the course of our business dealings. That was because I was a potential customer – he wanted the *Express* titles to be printed under contract at his Watford printing works and to distribute the *Express* titles jointly with Mirror Group titles, and I had been assigned by Stevens to evaluate the proposal.

Maxwell, accompanied by John Holloran, the boss of the Mirror print works, arrived at our Fleet Street building to do a presentation to

Stevens, myself and others of the *Express* team. Maxwell had one hell of a presence, and arrived carrying a large piece of cardboard under his arm. At the appropriate moment in the presentation he turned it round – it was a huge dummy cheque for £10 million. 'This can be yours,' he boomed, 'if you print with us.' At the time we were examining many options for our future print plans in the wake of the Fleet Street revolution, and Maxwell's option looked attractive on the surface.

We would not have to build a new plant; Maxwell would employ the print workers, so all our problems with print and distribution would miraculously disappear into his safe hands. However, when we started to evaluate the proposal it was pretty obvious that it was the usual Maxwell scamboli. Basically we were to pay for everything, including the interest on the *Mirror's* investment in new presses. Every print variation was to be an extra charge. We would have to pay for all redundancies but would have no control over the numbers of workers to be laid off or the redundancy terms. By the time we reached the bottom line, the Maxwell scheme would have cost us £10 million a year more than our own carefully costed plans.

I went to see Stevens and explained it to him in detail. He phoned Maxwell in front of me and blew him out. Maxwell was furious as he had been banking on the deal for dramatically cutting his own costs – at our expense. Stevens also told me that although he liked Maxwell he never really trusted him, and that if we had printed with him he had no doubt in the case of a crisis whose newspapers would be chucked off the back of the trucks first.

David Stevens was a curious mix. He could be amusing and very quick. He could be vain and sometimes vindictive. I hope he had a lot of fun running a newspaper group. But I don't think he really ever liked newspapers, the people who worked for them or what made the business tick.

In one newspaper interview a journalist asked him what advantages came from running a newspaper group. Stevens turned to the interviewer and asked, 'What did you call me?' 'Why ... Lord Stevens,' replied the slightly bemused reporter.

Lord Stevens smiled.

6

THE PEER AND
THE PORN KING

THERE HAS BEEN much speculation about the grimmest period in the *Daily Star*'s history, under Lord Stevens's chairmanship and my managing directorship, when we flirted with the Porn King, David Sullivan. The brief affair lasted barely six weeks during which time sales of the *Daily Star* dropped by more than 500,000 copies – almost a half its sale – and damaged the paper to such an extent that it has never really recovered.

Let me put the record straight, for I was present at every meeting which took place between the principals. The relationship between Lord Stevens, the peer, and David Sullivan, publisher of the *Sunday Sport* as well as top-shelf magazines such as *Razzle* and *Readers' Wives*, began for what seemed all the right reasons. The players in this sorry tale were Lord Stevens, Sir Gordon Linacre, his deputy chairman at United Newspapers, myself, David Sullivan and Michael Gabbert who, under the deal, was to be appointed editor of the *Daily Star*.

There was great concern at the United Newspapers board about the falling sales of the *Daily Star* under the latter period of Lloyd Turner's editorship. The *Daily Star* had started to become very worthy and caring, which was frankly not a good formula for a down-market tabloid, and the paper was no longer providing its readers with much of a sense of fun. Turner started to be a little bit like an actor, who having made his name in *Carry On* films, believes his great talent is worth more and starts to play Hamlet to tiny audiences. The time was rapidly approaching for a change of editor.

About this time, one of United's regional managing directors in Northampton approached Sir Gordon Linacre, his ultimate boss in the regions, with an almost unbelievable story. He claimed that David Sullivan was negotiating with Associated Newspapers, *Express*'s bitter rival in the mid-market, so that they would become involved with the *Sunday Sport* title and launch a daily version into the bottom end of the tabloid market.

There could only be one reason for doing this, apart from the fact that they had long had a hankering for owning a down-market title, and that was to use their great publishing expertise and buckets of money to attack the *Daily Star* which was highly vulnerable and which they no doubt saw as the soft underbelly of the Express Group.

An urgent council of war was called at United. After all, the *Daily Star* was picking up millions of pounds in overhead charges from the *Daily Express* and *Sunday Express*. The entire company could be in danger if the weight of another national newspaper publisher was to be thrown behind launching a daily version of the *Sunday Sport*, a spicy, rather over-the-top but reasonably successful down-market tabloid.

A meeting was sought with David Sullivan, proprietor of the *Sunday Sport*, who confirmed the rumour but claimed he was not unwilling to discuss alternatives as no contracts had yet been signed. Negotiations took place in the third-floor boardroom of the black glass building in Fleet Street. I found David Sullivan absolutely straight in his commercial dealings. If he agreed it, it was done. He was as good as his word.

Sullivan grew up in a council house in Wales. As a child he prayed for three wishes. The first was to be captain of Cardiff and Wales. The second was to become a world champion boxer and, if all else failed, to earn enough dosh to become a millionaire. He moved to South Yemen, where his father had moved to work, when he was ten – then he returned to the UK to go to boarding school

His first job was as a trainee advertising account executive, selling dog-food, which earned him £1500 a year. Then he met a man who was working part-time selling girlie mags. Within six months he was earning £35 a week at his full-time job and picking up £800 a week for his part-time activities. Over the next few years he was to go on to build an empire with an estimated 170 sex shops and titles like *Private*, *Climax*, *Romp* and *Whitehouse*.

Sullivan's all-time low was in 1982 when he was found guilty of living off immoral earnings through his ownership of a massage parlour. He ended up in jail – first in Wormwood Scrubs and then in Ford Open Prison: 'I spent seventy-one days in prison. Ten weeks and a day ... yeah, with hardened criminals.' The prisoners – most of them readers of his magazines – showed him 'massive respect'. They were convinced, he said, that he didn't belong there. Says Sullivan: 'The night before I'm coming up for my appeal, there's all the guards readin' my books ... and I thought ... This is a joke. They're all my customers.'

Sullivan was attracted to our proposals for they gave him considerable involvement in the future of the *Daily Star*. At the same time the deal meant that he didn't have to commit resources to the launch of his own daily newspaper, something he eventually did successfully on his own. (He later told me that he made money from issue one of the *Daily Sport*.) Under our deal Sullivan was to be appointed adviser on promotion and publicity, and we were to appoint his man, Gabbert, as editor of the *Daily Star*.

Stevens, Linacre and myself interviewed the candidate editor. I was then asked to see him on my own which I did one evening at Sullivan's flat opposite Hyde Park on the Bayswater Road. Apart from a distinctly sticky handshake, Gabbert was voluble, to say the least: it was hard to get a word in edgeways. He seemed bright, bouncy and full of ideas. It was only later that I grew to realise that he was a raging sex maniac and gutter rat.

He spoke of putting more 'pazzaz' into the paper, making it more fun, young, with more pop music, fashion and sport. I spent a couple of hours listening to him, and when I returned to the office, I wrote a not very helpful note to Stevens and Linacre saying that Gabbert would either be a raging success or an unmitigated disaster – there could be no middle ground.

It was decided to take the risk, and he was appointed with a huge salary by the standards of the mid-1980s and a large Mercedes car. The deal having been done, Gabbert was installed as editor in the *Star*'s Manchester editorial headquarters.

Michael Gabbert was the archetypal sleaze journalist, a man for whom the phrase and the world of 'gutter journalism' might have been invented. He didn't wear a grubby mac and a battered trilby with a 'Press' card stuck in the hatband. In most other aspects, however, he was the low-life investigative tabloid journalist out of Screen Casting – utterly amoral, with no discernible principles and even fewer scruples in pursuit of the only gods he ever worshipped – Big Money and B-I-G exclusives.

In spite of, and probably because of, these character defects, Gabbert was already a legend in the world of tabloid journalism. Colleagues and rivals alike spoke with grudging respect of his coups, and of the sharp and dirty tricks he had pulled to secure them.

Physically, Gabbert looked the part of a denizen of the underworld. A fleshy, unhealthy-looking man, his pasty, thick bespectacled face appeared a stranger to sunlight. His own appetites and weaknesses were often those of his victims for he was the newspaper gamekeeper who was still a poacher at heart.

Gabbert uncovered the villains and scoundrels not only because he knew them and where to find them, but, as likely as not, had often done business with them for either personal or professional reasons, or both.

He rose to newspaper fame on the back of one of the undeniably great exclusives of the early 1960s – the *Sunday People's* exposure of bribe-taking Sheffield Wednesday footballers. Gabbert was at that time the paper's northern news editor, based in Manchester, and he masterminded the investigation (though most of the work was done by a colleague, Trevor Kempson). But it was Gabbert who grabbed all the glory, and it was at this time that Ray Mills, later deputy editor of the *Daily Star*, saw him revelling in his success. Says Mills:

At that time Gabbert was living in a big, three- to four-storey Edwardian house in Didsbury and he threw a party to which every villain and hack in the North seemed to have been invited. When I got there, the place was heaving, the music loud, as loud as the women, but there was no sign of our host. I asked where he was and was pointed to a door at the top of the stairs.

So I knocked and went in – to find that it wasn't only the party that was heaving ... Gabbert was atop a girl and clearly in the final throes. 'Oh, sorry,' I said and retreated embarrassedly. But Gabbert was unfazed. 'Don't go,' he said, 'I won't be a minute.' And he wasn't. But, says Mills, 'I've never forgotten watching mesmerised as Gabbert's flabby white buttocks rose and fell as he finished his sexual business. Then he got up and asked if I 'wanted a go' on the object of his sated desires! I declined ...'

Fresh from the soccer bribes triumph, Gabbert switched to the opposition, the *News of the World*, then as now the biggest circulation Sunday paper of them all and also the paper that invented sleaze before the word had been coined. In many ways it was his natural home; the paper whose fearless investigators famously made their excuses and left when some sad tart offered the undercover men sexual services of many and varied kinds.

Often these offers were made as a barter for the silence of the reporter, and thus the paper, not the girls, lost the gamble on a Gabbert investigation – according to his fellow hacks on the 'Screws', Gabbert regularly availed himself of the offers, then mercilessly went ahead and exposed the girls anyway. Said one of his former colleagues: 'He was the *News of the World* man who made no excuses, and came.'

On the strength of the soccer bribes probe, Gabbert had been poached by the *News of the World* to head the paper's investigative team, and was given an assistant editor title. But while he was an acknowledged expert at pushing a story to its limits, and then beyond them, his methods and his habits often appalled even those colleagues whose own professional lives were spent exploring the darker side of human nature.

'Nowadays people talk about spin doctors as if it is something new,' says a *News of the World* journalist, 'but Mike was at it 30 years ago. He'd give a story what we call "top-spin", and if he had to doctor it to do so, that's what happened.'

His role as investigations supremo also gave him the power to explore further venalities (though he still cruised the streets in a big Mercedes, kerb crawling for girls who might satisfy his personal or professional needs). His reporters were often sent to get their boss supplies of cocaine, at a time when this drug was by no means as fashionable as it is today, and lurid stories were told of Gabbert's Cheshire

Cheese parties, where the top room of this famous old Fleet Street pub was hired for sex, drug and drink parties of unbridled licentiousness.

Gabbert's position also allowed him virtual freedom to exploit the *News of the World*'s seemingly bottomless pocket, and he was not slow to cash in on the fact that he could commission stories and pay freelance journalists for days or weeks of 'investigation' on mysterious stories which were known only to him.

Very soon, the Fleet Street gossip factory was humming with tales of how to get stories into the *News of the World*. A freelance, so it was said, only had to make a pitch to Gabbert and he would commission the story, or hire the freelance for further investigation, 'on the usual terms'. And everybody knew what Gabbert's 'usual terms' were – a thick backhander into Gabbert's wallet from the lavish fees which the *News of the World* paid ... on Gabbert's own authorisation.

By the early 1970s, Gabbert's methods had become too much for even the *News of the World* to swallow. Stafford Summerfield, the legendary editor, had gone in the wake of the Rupert Murdoch take-over in 1969 which launched the then young Aussie on his path to global domination. (Summerfield, who famously declared 'My mother always told me "never resign"', never got the choice.)

Gabbert felt he should have got Summerfield's job and was mightily displeased when it went instead to an old-stager C. J. 'Tiny' Lear, an amiable giant of a man.

Gabbert's fears were well founded; 'Tiny' didn't play the journalism game by Gabbert's rules and was basically a decent man who was increasingly disturbed as Gabbert's methods and habits filtered back to him.

Soon he decided that enough was definitely enough, and the last straw came when Gabbert's greed pushed him one step too far. He authorised and paid a fat fee for the times – the figure of £7000 was most commonly mentioned – to a girl 'freelance' whose journalistic skills were not as obvious as her sexual talents; in fact she was his current girlfriend.

'Tiny' was outraged when told of Gabbert's latest excess. He sought and got Murdoch's permission to sack him – and that was the end of Gabbert's first Fleet Street career.

Gabbert started his brief tenure of office as David Sullivan's nominated editor of the *Daily Star* as he meant to go on. He was appointed at the beginning of September 1987 and flew up to the paper's Manchester production HQ with its deputy editor, Ray Mills (who had already been appointed by me to oversee the Express Group's transition to direct input technology).

The new editor was bearing a huge envelope stuffed with 20in by 16in topless pictures of a young girl which he had commandeered from the *Sunday Sport*. One by one, almost sensuously, says Mills, he extracted the giant prints from the envelope and held them up for Mills – and the other stunned passengers on the shuttle flight – to view. The girl, an Anglo-Asian, was pretty enough, but her looks were almost a secondary consideration. What took Mills's and the other plane passengers' breath away was her truly titanic breasts, huge mammaries – entirely out of proportion to the girl's otherwise slim figure.

'How about that then?' enthused Gabbert. 'What a pair, eh!' Mills admitted that the girl's frontage was certainly spectacular. But the knockout blow was yet to come.

'Know how old she is?' asked Gabbert. Mills ventured to surmise about eighteen to twenty years.

'Nah,' said Gabbert dismissively. 'She's only fifteen. FIFTEEN!'

Mills was silent. There was an unwritten, but nonetheless accepted code on both the *Sun* and the *Star*, that topless girls had to be at least sixteen and Mills ventured, 'She's too young, Mike.' Gabbert was not-quite-about to breach that code. 'No, we're alright,' he said. 'She's sixteen next week, so we'll run pictures of her wearing a bit up top tomorrow and for a few days – and ask the punters whether she should get her kit off for her birthday!'

Given the evidence in front of him, Mills realised that the question for *Star* readers would be entirely rhetorical. And so of course it proved – Mike Gabbert announced his editorship the next day with a page-one picture of fifteen-year-old Natalie Banus baring almost all, and the next week she was inevitably pictured totally topless (at the alleged request of 'thousands' of *Daily Star* readers).

That evening, as the paper was being prepared and Natalie Banus was heading towards tatty immortality, Mills was in the office pub gloomily contemplating the future of a paper which was clearly heading from sauce to smut when he was joined by the news editor, Jeff McGowan. 'What's he going to do with it?' asked McGowan, a stalwart who had been with the *Star* since its birth. Mills sought the phrase which could sum up the new man's editorial philosophy, and recalled his own summation of his task on the flight to Manchester.

'He says,' said Mills, 'that we've got to produce a paper that's worth a wank on a wet weekend in Wigan.'

And this, it has to be said, was to be the summit of Gabbert's achievement.

Old habits did not die hard during Gabbert's time at the *Star*. In fact they didn't die at all. One afternoon, soon after Gabbert took over, Ray Mills paid a flying visit to Manchester and was sitting at the editor's desk when Gabbert was out of the room. Idly he pulled open a top drawer – and found it stuffed to bursting point with calculators, mini tape recorders, pens of all description and all the paraphernalia with which desk-bound staff surround themselves.

Enquiry about the hoard revealed that Gabbert was already known for his kleptomania among his colleagues. Anything that was left on a desk was fair game for this human magpie, and the staff had already learned to clutch their belongings to their bosoms whenever he hove into view.

It was possible to feel some sympathy for Gabbert at the *Star*, for he was the servant of two masters with diametrically opposed views of what the paper should be printing. Visible evidence of this were the two fax machines in his office, one linked directly to David Sullivan at his Roldvale porn HQ, the other to the *Express* in London.

The 'Sullivan' fax was rarely silent. The man was a fax maniac and sent a seemingly endless stream of requests, instructions and often bizarre demands from his Essex home. The *Express* fax was busy too, as we became increasingly alarmed at the editorial plunge down-market and the circulation slide.

Gabbert summed up the mutually exclusive demands made on him when he ripped two messages from the Sullivan and *Express* fax machines and brandished them at his editorial executives during an afternoon conference. 'Look at these,' he said. 'One from David Sullivan asking why we didn't have more topless tarts in today's paper, and why there wasn't more sex, and this is from Cameron complaining that there's too much sex and nudity.'

'I mean what the fuck am I supposed to do? I can't win.'

Circulation began to drop like a stone and it was soon in freefall with 500,000 copies rapidly lost off the daily sales. Major advertising agencies withdrew their top clients, especially the big retailers – Tesco was one of the first – whose customers were mainly women. (Some 30 per cent of *Star* readers were women.)

I saw David Stevens and we agreed that enough was enough. I would telephone Sullivan and give him the news. I was to break the deal which had been signed for five years. It had been running for just six weeks. From a sales conference in Jersey, I phoned Sullivan's Chigwell home to discover he was on his way to the US to watch one of his racehorses run, and was at Heathrow airport – I managed to get him paged, and he came to the phone in the first-class lounge. I gave him the news which left him stunned.

The following day, Stevens, Linacre and I saw Gabbert at United Newspapers' offices in Tudor Street. 'Sit down,' said Stevens. 'Have a cigar.' Gabbert took a large cigar, cut it, lit it and as he started to puff it, Stevens said, 'You're fired!' The whole deal was settled with Sullivan for a cash payment of over £1 million. After all, there was no legal reason to break the contract.

The poor *Daily Star*, the real victim in this saga, took years to stabilise its decimated sales which never really recovered, though under Brian Hitchen's editorship it made great strides as a 'proper' tabloid newspaper, and in due course the advertisers started to return. When I telephoned Brian to offer him the job he was on holiday in Spain, and apart from asking for lots of money, which I gave him, he asked me if he could have a Jaguar car which I also gave him; for years afterwards, however, he berated me about the fact that it didn't have 'proper leather seats', appropriate to his station in life.

A deal was struck, and the *Daily Star* was, once again, in safe hands.

7

THE ADFOLK
Sex, Scandals and Spies

IT IS ARGUABLE that nowhere in the newspaper world is the competition fiercer than among the men and women of the advertising departments. Pressure and stress are their constant companions. Their lives are dominated by targets; deadlines to meet, revenue to earn, percentages to fill, discounts to give, deals to make … every day, in every way, competition is the name of their game.

Their role is vital, for although the days are now gone where advertising revenue provided the biggest share of money required to produce a national newspaper, the contribution of the advertising departments is still critical, providing around 50 per cent of the revenue across seven days of publishing. The financial health of an individual newspaper or group depends on them. The cover price (minus wholesaler and retailer discounts), multiplied by the number of copies sold may provide a newspaper's bread and butter. Whether or not there is any jam, and how thickly such available jam is spread, depends largely on the admen and women.

Advertising folk live in the fast lane. They live hard, they work hard and they play hard – and sometimes they fiddle too! And on a scale which would put the average expenses-cheating hack to shame.

My first taste of a newspaper advertising department had been as a 27-year-old when I joined the advertising department of the London *Evening Standard.* whose ad director at the time was the aforementioned Colin Owen-Browne. I couldn't have had a better tutor and taskmaster. Colin was an unusual individual, years ahead of his time in terms of ad selling, who tragically died at the early age of 42, leaving a young family. It always comes as a shock to me when characters who appear larger than life have their mortality proved in such an awful way.

Colin saw himself as an inspirational leader. Our sales meetings were always tinged with military activity. 'The North Vietnamese are coming over the top at you!' he exhorted (it was at the height of the Vietnam War).

Once he got so carried away that he pushed his chair over backwards, leaving only his legs waving above the desk while continuing to berate the wretched North Vietnamese as he shouted to be picked up. When order was restored he had the style to continue as though nothing had happened despite the murmur of stifled hysteria around the room.

Colin was intensely interested in the sexual activities of his department, which employed around two hundred souls, many of them very attractive young women. He was a great believer in 'staff motivation' and encouraged bonuses and team-building activities such as river-boat discos. These provided a special problem for no husbands, wives or partners were allowed – only staff. Booze would flow freely and by the time the boat docked friendships, however temporary, would have been forged through the alcoholic haze, many to be regretted much later. Next day the inquisition would start. Owen-Browne would quiz each manager on who went home with whom. All would be remembered for future use.

After one such event all those with cars were asked to drop off colleagues going in their general homeward direction. I was commandeered to take five people to drop en route to my home in Kent.

The last to be dropped was a pneumatic young woman in the secretarial pool. When we arrived at some anonymous Lewisham estate, she asked not to be dropped outside her house because her husband had left the back door open. We drove round to the garage in the cul-de-sac behind the house and stopped. After a moment she asked, 'Well, are you going to do anything?' I replied, 'I'm certainly not.'

The abuse was awful. 'One day you'll be old and nobody will want you!' she screamed. She leapt out of the car and ran to the back door of her house.

In the office the next day she was all sweetness and light. It was as though nothing had happened which, indeed, was true.

Yet in the advertising department for which I was later to be responsible as managing director, a lot of things happened and they were to give me many a sleepless night.

Three of the biggest scandals to shake Express Newspapers in my time involved advertising executives. Money, ambition, greed and sex all played their part in the departure of three successive high-flying admen.

The first to go was David Lammin, advertising director of the *Daily Express* in Jocelyn Stevens's day. Lammin was caught out in the early 1980s on a fairly routine fiddle which involved using space in the *Express* titles to promote one of his personal sidelines. Basically, he owned caravans in the south of France which he rented out, and vacant weeks were advertised in the ad columns.

Nothing wrong with that except Lammin never offered to pay, even at a 'staff' discount rate, for the space he had hijacked. (Not surprisingly, he neglected to tell anyone he had used the *Express* purchasing department to have his personal business note paper and stationery printed at the company's expense.)

Taxed with the evidence, David Lammin held his hands up, admitted it was 'a fair cop' and departed with as good grace as he could muster with the whole affair turning out to be a nine-day-wonder which few outside the advertising department either knew or cared about.

But the man who 'fingered' Lammin and plunged the knife up to the hilt in his boss's back was to figure prominently in the next two scandals to rock the *Express* advertising boat.

Stan Myerson was the 'grass' who sneaked – sleek, saturnine, immaculately and expensively dressed – he was the very model of a modern, thrusting, ambitious adman. Charming or ruthless as the occasion demanded, Myerson's vaulting ambition knew few bounds, and I doubt that he had any second thoughts about his decision to turn his boss in when he found out about Lammin's peccadilloes.

Colouring his judgement may well have been the calculation that he might get his boss's job, for Myerson was at the time deputy adver-tisement director of the *Daily Express* and had good reason to believe that he would be the prime candidate to replace the disgraced Lammin. After all, he had been with the *Express* for at least five years and was undoubtedly the star player in the *Express* ad world of snakes and ladders. But if this was the Myerson game plan, it misfired – just as it was to fail again ten years later in similar circumstances.

Certainly Lammin had to go – no matter how much or how little money was involved. The fact that a director misused his company's resources for personal gain made his departure inevitable. But the manner in which he was 'shopped' inevitably left a sour taste, and perhaps this is why Stan Myerson's gamble on his own future didn't quite work out in the way he may have planned it. He also omitted to allow for Lammin's popularity with the then deputy managing director, Mike Murphy. Murphy had a caravan close to Lammin's south of France operation, and they were good friends.

Myerson's action in reporting Lammin's malfeasances was initially seen as that of a conscientious corporate officer concerned to keep the good name of the company unsullied. But was this his only concern, and was he really the man to replace his victim? Perhaps not: in any event, Myerson did not get the foreman's job.

Instead, the company headhunted outside its own 'nest of vipers' and brought in Michael Moore from TV AM, where for a short time he had been general manager of the ailing breakfast station, while Myerson had to console himself with the number two job as deputy advertisement director.

Moore had made his name working in Rupert Murdoch's empire, and being every bit as bright and tough as you might expect from a Murdoch henchman, he seemed more than a match for his deputy. Together they made a formidable team, and soon the ad team were firing on all cylinders. The two of them set the department buzzing and helped create a great 'feel good' atmosphere for everyone working in the place. This partnership was to last more than ten years, although it started to fall apart dramatically towards the end. For Moore, too, the man to exploit any weakness was always right behind him.

The lid suddenly came off the can of advertising worms early in 1995 when Moore was on holiday and Myerson was running the ad department. He asked to see me on a 'personal' matter. Given that I knew Myerson had long been conducting an in-office affair with a classified ad manager, and Moore's own interest in the opposite sex was heavily rumoured, my heart sank at the prospect of yet more unsavoury revelations.

My fears were well justified. Myerson told me that Moore had approached his wife, Clare, at an industry function and had insidiously started to plant the seeds of doubt in his deputy's wife's mind. 'Where do you think Stan is tonight?' he asked Clare, leaving her in little doubt that she might not like the answer to his rhetorical question. And then, apparently, Myerson claimed Moore played the 'agony uncle' card, telling Clare consolingly that 'you can always talk to me about it'.

That at least, was Myerson's version of the story and it was not good news. To have the advertising director and his deputy so clearly at each other's throats was prejudicial to good order and discipline.

On his return from holiday Moore came to see me and insisted that I should sack Myerson for serious breaches of his role in terms of his attitude to staff. He was bullying them unmercifully, Moore said, and would have to go for the good of the company. I was at a loss. So far as the company was concerned, Myerson was much respected by his fellow directors, and was felt by all of them to be a natural successor should Moore ever decide to leave.

I was in a quandary; was it really part of a managing director's role to step in and adjudicate on the private lives of his executives? That in itself was a ticklish enough problem. I felt that as a first step I had to move Myerson out of Moore's firing line, so I created a role for him as 'assistant to the managing director', with responsibility for investigating business opportunities in electronic publishing. It was a non-job, but it was designed to buy time.

No sooner was Myserson safely out of the ad department than he dropped his next bombshell in the form of an allegation which made it inescapable that I should have to act firmly – and fast. His sensational claim was one of monumental fiddling by Moore, and on a scale which could neither be hidden nor ignored.

I pressed him strongly over the allegations – although I suspect it would not have needed any pressure at all – and he revealed a story of how Moore had cheated the company out of hundreds of thousands of pounds in what was known as 'contra dealing'. These deals involved giving an advertiser free or massively discounted space in exchange for substantial kickbacks which, according to Myerson, went straight into Moore's back pocket. Apparently the amount of space given away by Moore by that date amounted to a mind-boggling £600,000, he said.

I was horrified at the thought of such a scandal. Compared with these allegations, the sexual frolics of the ad director and his deputy paled. But where was the evidence for the corruption which Myerson alleged? Any malpractice would be difficult to prove, especially, as I had to assume, that both Moore and the advertiser involved would strongly deny malpractice. Since such an arrangement would obviously not involve paperwork of any kind, trying to prove anything would be an uphill struggle.

It was at this stage that I took a decision I was later to regret; a decision that eventually led to our actions being splashed over three pages in the *Mail on Sunday*, which revelled in our embarrassment.

Myerson told me that the managing director of the company concerned in the advertising scam was coming into the office to negotiate his annual advertising contract directly with Michael Moore, and I took advice on how best to try to trap Moore into unwittingly confirming the allegations. The consensus of opinion was that we should attempt to get Moore to incriminate himself – out of his own lips. In other words, bug his office and tape his conversation with his alleged partner in crime.

It was a deeply repugnant decision. The whole idea of electronic eavesdropping on a colleague and fellow director was anathema to me. But at the time it seemed to offer a way of conclusively settling the affair, and, reluctantly, I gave the go-ahead to hire a security firm who specialised in such shadowy surveillance work.

Because of his knowledge of the 'scam', Myerson was part of the 'bug implant' team. They wired up Moore's office, even concealing a microphone in one of the potted plants which decorated his working area. (This is why, when *Private Eye* later published their version of events, staff throughout the building were said to have been seen muttering into potted foliage and whispering, 'I'm just having a word with Cameron'.) In retrospect, it did have its rather hilarious side although, at the time, I didn't see much to laugh about.

I would happily have settled for some personal embarrassment if my scheme had worked as planned. But it didn't. Moore's meeting with his alleged fellow conspirator went ahead. The problem lay in the fact that the tapes of those conversations were blurred and indistinct, and the few passages that could be clearly heard proved that no nefarious dealings were going on at all and provided only a record of a straightforward business discussion.

I was relieved to find that there was no evidence of wrongdoing by our advertising director, but I still had to deal with Myerson. I sent for him and told him that there appeared to be no substance to his allegations and that Moore's private life (and indeed, Myerson's private life) could be of no concern to me if they did not affect the well-being of the company.

Of course, I knew that I would soon have to tackle the obviously bitter feud between the two of them, but Myerson took the matter out of my hands. His reaction to my 'hands off' approach was almost frightening in its ferocity. 'If you can't prove it I will,' he vowed, and left my office obviously seething with resentment, rage and frustration.

Myerson's vengeance was not long in coming. Having failed to nail Moore on the grounds of financial corruption, he turned, inevitably it seemed, to his boss's private life.

Just as I had, Myerson turned for outside assistance to seek the evidence – any evidence – which would serve to get rid of his hated rival. He hired a firm of private detectives nominally at his own expense. In fact, they were hired on company notepaper and when the firm became curious about why they had not been paid they came after us, believing Myerson had been acting on the company's behalf. We were lumbered with the bill. Among other things, it seemed strange behaviour for a man who regularly claimed to be the son of a multi-millionaire.

The mission of Myerson's private eyes was to shadow Moore and follow him to Manchester, where he was hosting the *Express* advertising department's summer party, an event laid on to woo existing and potential advertisers – an important event especially since the *Express* had closed its northern sales office some years previously.

It was an annual wing-ding which involved Moore and his entourage staying overnight at the Mereside Hotel, near where the function was held. Myerson either knew, or guessed, that his boss would take the opportunity to get up to no good, and so it proved.

A few days later, Myerson asked to see me, walked triumphantly into my office and hurled the report of the private detectives on to my desk. Moore had unwittingly played right into Myerson's hands – and into the knickers of a married classified ads manager who had succumbed to his rampant charms.

The report admitted of no other conclusion. It detailed how Moore had wooed the woman, then arranged for her to come to his bedroom. As dawn broke hours later, he had ushered her from his room wearing only his underpants. It was the detail of the underpants that clinched it for me. They were made, reported the diligent private dick, in a Rupert Bear pattern; a detail that simply couldn't have been invented and which, as W. S. Gilbert might have said, added verisimilitude to an otherwise bald but convincing narrative.

Poor Rupert Bear – stalwart of the *Daily Express* since Beaver-brook's day; who would have thought that the cartoon character of such inoffensive innocence would play a part in the downfall of the *Express*'s advertising supremo?

'Now will you do something?' demanded the exultant Myerson, clearly expecting that I would sack the feckless Moore within minutes. But it was by no means as simple as that.

Moore's frolicking was undeniably interesting, but what did that have to do with me, or the company? The man was entitled to a private life, however unsavoury that might be in some people's eyes. And if we started sacking people for having 'a bit on the side', as it might be crudely expressed, where would it all end? It didn't need even a moment's thought to see an endless chain of wrongful dismissal claims inevitably following, not to mention a much reduced work force.

The Moore report only proved – if proof were needed – that our advertising director was vigorously heterosexual with a dubious taste in underpants. So I told Myerson the situation had not changed at all, and he left in high dudgeon. But in fact the situation had changed and initially it seemed that Myerson's master plan had worked. In the circumstances I felt that I had to tell Mike Moore what had been going on and so I sent for him and showed him the report.

Inevitably, Moore was embarrassed and discomfited by the revelations, not only because he had been caught with his pants down (or up as the private dicks noted), but also because his former deputy had gone to such lengths to seek his downfall. He told me that he felt he had to resign because he believed that if he did not, Myerson would send the report to his wife. Myerson had already told me that he intended to do just that unless Moore resigned.

So Michael Moore fell on his sword, essentially as a result of being blackmailed by Myerson. He left Express Newspapers shortly after his tenth anniversary with the company, with a handsome pay-off which not only recognised the undoubted energy and dynamism he had put into his department, but also the fact that he had never failed to meet his budgets. It also reflected the fact that, although suspicions about his financial methods would not go away, we had failed to prove wrongdoing or malpractice. Moore eventually became the managing director of *The European* newspaper, and I was delighted for him. But if he were to go to his grave believing himself a victim of Stan Myerson, I wouldn't blame him; and I can guess what his last wishes would be.

If Mike Moore had any faint hopes that by resigning he would avoid damaging publicity, these hopes were soon dashed

A few weeks after his departure, the story of Moore's mucky weekend in Manchester, even down to the Rupert Bear underpants, and pictures of Moore and his paramour were spread over three pages in the *Mail on Sunday*, who were delighted to swallow Myerson's tale of corruption at the *Express*. He was a very plausible fellow indeed.

But Myerson's triumph at Moore's downfall was short-lived. All Myerson's plotting against his boss started to rebound on him because it made senior management start to look very closely at the man himself and his activities in the ad department, whereupon a great deal of dirt began to float to the surface.

For years Myerson had promoted an inflated account of himself and his background. He claimed to come from a hugely wealthy South African family and that his father employed tens of thousands of people, any or all of whom could be fired at will for misbehaviour; indeed, he told me on one occasion, they could go missing ... and left me to jump to the desired conclusion.

Well, perhaps Myerson senior could make some employees who crossed him disappear without trace. Or perhaps ... Our freelance reporters in South Africa seemed to think that his draper's shop in

Johannesburg might have been a little crowded if it contained the tens of thousands of staff that Myerson junior claimed his father employed.

Indeed, Myerson told me that when his marriage was on the rocks because of Moore's interference, there were family trusts in favour of his children which would have to be unwound. Millions of pounds were involved, and teams of barristers and accountants were working on the problem.

As we dug deeper into the Mysersons' affairs we found it curious that Clare Myerson had never heard of such trusts. Moreover, she claimed that her husband's mother and father always travelled to England tourist class, and that she had never seen any signs of wealth when she had visited them in South Africa. Moreover, she strenuously denied a claim by Myerson that she had flown to South Africa to help sort out the problems with the children's trusts.

At all events, suspicion about Myerson and his antecedents was such that he once gave me a fax number in Jo'burg which he claimed was his father's. This followed rumours that his father was going to fly over and address the investment community in the City of London about corruption at the *Express*, using his millions to emphasise the point. He gave me the fax number to contact his father to determine what exactly he planned to do.

I wrote to his father saying how ridiculous I felt his plan was. Sure enough, a fax came back fully supporting his son's story. And yet ... and yet; was the fax number really from Myerson senior? Was the reply, on cheap, unheaded notepaper, really from the man himself? And would a man as mega-wealthy as Myerson claimed really be operating from a flat in Jo'burg?

The doubts persisted, but idle curiosity about whether Myerson was everything he claimed to be was soon overshadowed by the volume of evidence that began to accumulate about the man and his methods.

And it became clear that far from Moore being the arch-villain of the piece, Myerson would be much better cast in the role.

For a start, it was well known that Myerson was guilty of the very 'offence' which eventually brought about Moore's downfall – that of extra-marital dallying. Myerson had been married for some years to Clare, a former editorial secretary at the *Express* and a delightful person, who was apparently totally unaware that her husband was having a long-term affair with a girl who was a classified ads manager named Rene Hoenderkamp.

In business terms, the fact of their affair was just as immaterial as it had been in Moore's case; but his mistress's position in the classified ads section allowed him to feather both their nests at the company's expense.

It was a neat scam and based on bonuses which play a vital part in selling advertisements. Bonuses are a very valuable incentive, and ad sales people who bring in and clinch their weekly sales budgets are rewarded with lumps of cash which can be very substantial indeed. The bonuses for the classified department are assessed separately from the display department, but targets and bonuses for both departments are under the control of the ad director or, of course, his deputy.

This is where Myerson was in a position to 'help' both himself and his mistress. If classified sales were down on target, he could – and did – ensure that they were achieved by transferring revenue from the above target display ad sales figures. The result was a healthy bonus for Rene and her classified colleagues which they hadn't really earned, plus an even healthier bonus for Myerson himself because his bonus was based on the overall departmental performance. He could collect a maximum 50 per cent on top of his large annual salary.

It was purely an internal scam, for the ads would appear just as the advertiser or advertising agency had booked them, and they would be billed correctly. But the figures upon which the all-important bonuses were calculated would be diverted by the computer manager on the direct instructions of ... Stan Myerson.

In fact the computer manager, David Pring, realised exactly what was going on and was so terrified that at some stage he would have to carry the can that he kept the instructions he got from Myerson, lodged them in his bank, and produced them when the manure finally hit the fan.

Myerson didn't stop at electronic fiddling either. He was also fiddling his expenses on a grand scale, even bullying staff into filling in fictitious receipts and embroiling them in the corruption by encouraging them to climb on the bent expenses bandwagon and do just the same.

In fact, we realised that Myerson was ruling his department not just with a rod of iron, but through what amounted to a reign of terror. His rages were notorious and feared by all his staff without exception. The man who claimed to have been a boxing champion (though once again with little in the way of proof) had repeatedly threatened violence to his staff, and actually carried out his threats on some occasions, and many of them confessed that they were very afraid to talk about him.

Myerson knew that we had started to examine his role and had warned several of his senior staff that their jobs, their futures, and their physical well-being would be at risk if they talked to us. We had to give these people personal guarantees about their security before they could be persuaded to give us even a glimpse of the disturbing happenings in the advertisement department. Indeed I felt that this was the main but not the only reason; many of them had benefited, and been aware that they had benefited, from both the bonus and expenses scams.

On occasions, Myerson's frauds were simple but blatant. Once he breakfasted handsomely with his mistress and submitted the top half of

the bill with his expenses as spurious evidence that he had been entertaining some advertising bigwig or other. It was a fairly routine bit of
expenses padding but when the bottom half of the same bill emerged
in support of an entirely separate, and equally spurious, claim from
Rene, it was difficult to avoid the conclusion that Myerson and his lady
were treating the company with contempt.

Among the many skeletons in the Myerson cupboard was the case
of the media director whom Myerson claimed to have entertained
twice for lunch on the same day – once in the West End of London and
once in the East End.

In fact, this media director was something of a regular in Myerson's
fantasy world of expense account entertaining, His name appeared
often on the Myerson expense forms as being the recipient of generous
lunches, and I was so suspicious that I took the trouble to call the man
whose name was being taken in vain. Jocularly I congratulated him on
his evidently healthy appetite. He realised immediately the real purpose
of my call.

That year, he told me, he had lunch with Myerson twice and he had
paid for one of them! But these were just a few bricks in the monument
of deceit and intimidation which it was now clear Myerson had erected
around himself. His mistress had already been fired for her own
expenses fiddling, and it was now time – and well past time – to grasp
the Myerson nettle.

The volume of testimony we had accumulated made his dismissal
inevitable and long overdue, and the statistical evidence which the
computer systems man had locked away made his guilt on that account
alone incontrovertible.

Myerson was now fighting for his professional life as our enquiries
remorselessly proceeded. As the net closed in, his rages were fearsome
to behold. At one point he confronted my principal investigators,

administration director Struan Coupar and production director Paul Rudd, and exploded into such a paroxysm of anger that the two men feared for their safety. But in losing his rag so spectacularly, Myerson only hammered another nail into his coffin. The stories we had been picking up about his reign of terror sounded so appalling that we could not initially bring ourselves to believe them. Now it was all becoming only too credible.

Myerson saw that dismissal was inevitable, but he fought for at least the same deal as the man he had knifed. He claimed that he should have the same pay-off scale as Moore. He would accept defeat, but not dishonour. He threatened and pleaded, but all to no avail. We now knew the manner of man we were dealing with. There could be no question of compounding all our earlier misjudgements by letting him sneak away into the night with yet more money from the *Express* coffers which he had so cynically exploited over the years.

It was at this stage that the bully became the beggar. Now he started to whine about his financial hardships. The braggart who boasted about his £500,000 house and his millionaire background was examined by the Child Support Agency on behalf of Clare and their two children. The CSA, who are hardly known for their kid gloves examinations, reported at the conclusion of their investigations that he was unable to afford anything but minimal support. The house was not worth what he claimed. It was mortgaged to the hilt despite his having told everyone that he had 'bought it for cash'.

Myerson was sacked for gross misconduct, a charge which he vigorously denied. He went, kicking and screaming to the end, blaming everybody but himself, and vowing to fight his dismissal up to the highest court in the land.

In fact, he hired lawyers to act for him in a case of wrongful dismissal. But in the face of our refusal even to discuss a settlement out

Above and below: Where the newspaper trade came from! Overmanning at every position. (Note: many of the men are smoking amidst highly flammable materials.)

Left: Sir John Junor – 'a gia[nt] amongst pigmies'. (*Daily Mail*)

Below: Sir Jocelyn Stevens – a unique and effective manager. (Alan Davidson)

Above: Lord Matthews – who rose from shop floor to business leadership. (Ray Wright)

Above right: The author at the time of his appointment as Managing Director in 1986.

Right: Sir Larry Lamb – a distinguished editor who did not suffer any fool gladly. (*Daily Mail*)

Left: Planning meeting, 1987 in the Black Lubyanka, to discuss investment in the future. From left to right: Paul Sergeant, Ray Mills, Alan Bellinger, unknown, Tony Bentley, the author, Michael Moore, Nick Shott, Les Ivell, Robin Esser, Murdoch MacLennan (now MD at Associated Newspapers).

Right: Mike Gabbert – an investigative reporter without principles. (*Daily Mail*)

Right: David Sullivan – unscrupulous enterpreneur. (*Daily Mail*)

Left: Brian Hitchen –
journalist to editor, the
patriotic 'Brit.' (*Daily
Mail*)

Below: Sir Nicholas and
Lady Lloyd – 'the glitterati
of Fleet Street'. As Eve
Pollard, she was Editor of
the *Sunday Express*; he
was Editor of the *Daily
Express*. (Desmond O'Nei

Right: Richard
Addis – Editor of the
Daily Express,
plucked from the
middle ranks of the
Daily Mail. (*Daily
Mail*)

Right: The author
with Lord Stevens –
a ten-year
partnership.

Above: The author in his office at the new Express HQ in Blackfriars Road, across the River Thames from the City of London whose financial institutions so dominated British newspaper policy.

Below: The new Head Office building for United Newspapers and Express Newspapers, 1988.

of court, and after being aware of the evidence we had gathered, he eventually dropped the case having let us know that he had fired his lawyers and was representing himself. I suspect the lawyers parted with him. His own knowledge of the law was woeful, though another of his claims was that he had qualified as a barrister in South Africa, and sometimes signed himself LLB.

Stan Myerson was probably the most distasteful and unpleasant man I met in all my newspaper years. It is to my own discredit that I didn't realise his many failings until it was almost too late.

One intriguing mystery is why the Moore–Myerson partnership, which had worked so successfully for many years, fell apart in such an evil brew of duplicity and villainy. I have my own theory as to why the explosion took place after Myerson had worked for the company for seventeen years, ten of them closely with Michael Moore. I believe it was a case of the eternal triangle and that the truth might never have come out had it not been for two women.

Michael Moore's paramour was Lenia Michael, a girl who exuded sex appeal. She was a rising star in the classified department, had been rapidly promoted and was a very good sales manager. Rene Hoenderkamp, another long-serving manager and Myserson's mistress, also worked in the same department. Hoenderkamp lodged a formal complaint that Lenia Michael had been unfairly promoted and overpaid. The unsaid accusation was that this was due to Lenia's relationship with Moore. Myerson picked up the cudgels on Rene's behalf. Moore under another guise said Myerson had to go – leading to a bloody nightmare for the poor company and its managing director.

8

LESSONS IN CREATIVE WRITING

AT THE HEART of Fleet Street were ferocious deadlines, scoops and intense competition at all levels – between newspapers, within newspapers, among departments. But it was also a hotbed of affairs of the heart, tears and disappointments, depths of despair and great peaks of emotion. It was also a vipers' nest of corruption from many angles.

The avarice of the unions and the chicanery of the ad departments were matched by the nefarious activities of some journalists. Their particular brand of double dealing was centred on expenses fiddling, something they regarded as their natural right. Of course there were many journalists who did not participate (although on a rival paper a young journalist had her weekly expenses thrown back at her by her boss because they weren't large enough).

When corruption takes hold and becomes endemic it is inclined to become the 'norm' and must be extinguished at every opportunity. The journalist is in the ideal position to milk the system. There were 'tips' to contacts – with no receipts required; 'drinks' with contacts – once again, with no receipts necessary. Stories were commissioned from 'mates' which were paid for but never used. On occasions some journalist would be caught taking fat backhanders from those 'mates' out of the very money they had authorised in the company's name.

National newspapers operate in a highly pressurised and well-paid industry, both in editorial and in ad sales, and expenses were just another challenge. My rule on expenses fiddling was simple. If someone was caught with their sticky fingers in the till they were dismissed. There were no 'ifs' or 'buts', no matter how small the amount involved in the fiddle. Theft is theft. The alteration of a receipt from £6 to £60 was a typical example. The accountants were always on the look-out for dodgy receipts; sometimes the total had been altered. On other occasions the journalist would make a foolish mistake and a restaurant receipt would be submitted with the receipt number showing an earlier sequence to one already submitted some weeks before.

On discovery, the internal auditor would be dispatched to the restaurant concerned to take a sneaky look at the receipt pad or just ask the waiter when a particular receipt was issued. One of the advantages of VAT is that restaurants have to be pretty careful with their records.

Expense sheets were properly authorised by departmental superiors before submission. At each level the next senior journalist had to sign, then the process continued up to the editor who signed the most senior journalists' expense sheets. The reality was that having grown up through the system, each level of seniority also saw the system as a challenge when it came to their own expenses, and the biggest fiddles I came across were initiated by the most senior journalists, and sometimes by the editors themselves. Expenses in national newspapers have always been considered a challenge by all those entitled to claim them. In fact, in the case of journalists and admen, the target for some seemed to be to claim one's living expenses through expense claims and bank your salary.

I suspect a number achieved these heady heights despite the eagle eyes of the accountants. Occasionally someone would really be caught out, having pulled a scam which was often revealed only by a fluke. Once, a journalist and photographer were sent to Egypt to cover a river race of some sort. On their return they submitted a receipt for the hire of a fast speedboat, when in fact they had met up, by accident, with some British soldiers who were in Egypt undergoing some sort of aquatic training course. They just happened to have a fast speedboat, courtesy of Her Majesty's Government, which they were only too happy to provide to the intrepid journalists for the price of a few beers.

Months later, purely by chance, the photographer involved was having a beer with his picture editor at the Punch Tavern in Fleet Street when there was a mutual recognition across the bar. The guy who came over, unfortunately for the photographer, just happened to be one of the soldiers he had met in Egypt; and the soldier insisted on showing the photographer and his boss the happy snaps he had taken when the journalists borrowed the military craft!

There were literally hundreds of expense forms processed each week, and jumping on an individual and firing him or her was a sort of control system. It made others wary, for a short time anyway. All these expense forms had, of course, been properly authorised by several signatures, up to the editor or the ad director for the most senior people. The trouble was that if the signatory was also on the same bandwagon, the pot often had some difficulty in calling the kettle black. Indeed, on occasions a member of staff would be told to charge a meal or two as a reward for some service beyond the call of duty – a sort of tax-free backhander for the blue-eyed boys and girls. In many cases, where editors were concerned, I just put some of the more outrageous claims in my drawer where they remained. Not once did the subject get raised with me by the individual editor concerned.

Once, a country cottage was required for a photo-shoot. It so happened that an editor owned such a cottage and decided it was an ideal location for the shoot. Two weeks later I received an unreceipted claim for £600 from the editor for the use of the cottage. The editor had mentally justified it to himself, without discussion on the basis that the company would have had to pay for the location anyway, so why not pay him?

Editors were, of course, directors of the company, and therefore were bound by the rules of fiduciary duty. Fleet Street editors' salaries are pretty well known – rarely less than £150,000 a year, and frequently much higher – plus all the perks: Jaguar car, top of the range only, of course, with a chauffeur for their personal and business use. Then there are expensive lunches for everyone from their own chosen staff to cabinet ministers and pop stars. Editors' expense claims ran to literally hundreds of pounds a week. The Savoy Grill would probably go bankrupt without the contribution of editors. I always felt that when we appointed an editor, we gave him or her a crown of laurels which could scramble their brains. When perfectly normal people were suddenly thrust into the position of instant access to the great and good, it had a remarkable effect on their ego.

On one occasion the finance director brought me a dodgy claim from a senior journalist, the *Daily Express* medical correspondent. It was from an N1 curry house and had been altered in a very amateur fashion from £11 to £111: obviously a receipt from a take-away. His claim form detailed a glittering array of senior surgeons and consultants from the Royal London Hospital. Unfortunately for him, one of the surgeons, the head of Accident and Emergency at the Royal London is a personal friend of mine, and he and his wife happened to be dining at my house on that very night. As an aside, he cannot stand curry. Exit one red-faced and foolish journalist.

Over £5000 was misappropriated by one *Sunday Express* journalist. His claims were littered with fudged receipts over a twelve-month period. I sent for the editor and said the man was to be fired immediately, and I would also consider calling in the police. The individual admitted to his crimes, and the editor came back to me to plead for the man's job. The latter had offered to pay back the proceeds of his dishonesty in instalments, the editor said, if he could keep his job. It seemed to me that both the journalist and the editor had completely missed the point.

Probably the most innovative fiddles ever carried out were by a senior woman journalist on the *Daily Express* in Larry Lamb's era. She was very ingenious. Signing off expenses is a bit of a chore for a busy editor, and in the case of his senior staff the editor normally only gives the sheets a cursory glance when presented to him. If a fiddling executive picks the right busy moment, he or she may get away with blue murder.

Her expenses were always beautifully presented; typed up with all receipts correct. What nobody realised was that she was 'doubling up'. Three months later she would resubmit the same claim again. It was simple but effective. No busy person would remember who an individual had entertained after that amount of time, but some eagle eye in the accounts department smelled a rat, and as a result she promptly left our employ.

Another classic fiddle was foisted on the legendary person of John Junor by one of his leader writers. This man was a shopaholic and presumably this was the reason for his addiction to the expenses lottery. Well trusted by Junor, he would present his claim form folded over with only the signature box showing, and Junor would duly sign. What no one realised was that this man was completing an entirely new column and adding it to the total. Lord knows how long this had been going on for – possibly years – but it was apparent that thousands of pounds were involved.

One man asked to see me because he was in debt, and felt that the company might consider making him a loan. The usual sad reasons were enumerated: marriage breakdown, mortgage payments, a rented flat for himself and so on. The company did not, as a policy, make loans to staff, but what they did do was arrange for a senior member of the company's bank to see the individual and give financial advice, co-ordinate the creditors, and reschedule the debts into manageable repayments.

I asked the man what he owed, expecting the usual reply of a few thousand pounds at most. I nearly fell off my chair when he said £96,000. It was three-years' gross salary at his pay level. He even owed money to most of his colleagues. The bank officials were excellent. They contacted all the creditors and told them that it was better they got something over a long period than nothing if the man were to go bankrupt. For a year he was as good as gold, and met the minimum repayments. Then unfortunately, one Christmas, temptation presented itself with a vengeance. Because staff were paid monthly, at the end of the month, advances were offered at Christmas to cope with the inevitable financial load on individuals. He was advanced £500. Later that day he was passing the International Sporting Club. He went in and lost the lot and another £500 on credit trying to recoup his loss. Nobody knew, and he had neglected to tell us, that he was an inveterate gambler. This time he was beyond help.

I am absolutely sure that we only ever melted the very tip of the enormous iceberg of expense fiddles. At times, to switch metaphors, it was like trying to push water uphill with a rake. But we kept at it.

One of the most difficult cases involved one of our editors in Scotland, a long-serving journalist who was very well respected by the company, Scottish politicians and the Scottish establishment. He was frequently called upon to give his views on Scottish matters on TV and radio and, unbeknown to the company, set up his own news agency in Edinburgh. From this office he would not only take stories from other agencies but also commission them to carry out work, some of it fictitious, authorise the payments, and then accept a chunk of that money back in cash in some seedy pub.

It was a crime almost impossible to detect, but like all crimes, the culprit is usually discovered by one of the participants spilling the beans. In this case, the lady who ran the agency on the editor's behalf received a demand from the tax man on her earnings. It didn't take her long to realise that her tax bill included, as it would, tax on the payments she had handed over to the corrupt editor, and she was understandably most unhappy. She told a friend, who told someone else, and it then came to our ears. We identified at least £30,000 taken over a reasonably short period. It was probably much more.

9

JJ
A Flawed Legend

OF ALL THE EDITORS I knew and worked with at Express Newspapers, John Junor, editor of the *Sunday Express* for 32 years, towered above them all. He was a giant among pygmies, one of those few men of whom it could truly be said that he was a legend in his own lifetime, a man regarded with fear, respect or awe by those who crossed his path.

From 1954 to 1986, John Junor edited the *Sunday Express* and ran it as his personal fiefdom, tolerating interference from few, be they manager or proprietor. JJ, as he was known to journalists and readers alike, was a law unto himself; to all intents and purposes he *was* the *Sunday Express*, and his column was not only his voice but that of the paper itself.

Knighted in 1980 for his services to newspapers (and Margaret Thatcher), the trenchant and uncompromising views of this son of a Glasgow Calvinist steelworker were uncannily shared or reflected by millions of readers. He was both the body and soul of the paper and he spoke directly to and for that vast body of people now collectively known as Middle England.

John Junor inevitably plays a major role in the story of the triumphs and disasters of Express Newspapers if only because he was a central figure in the drama. He entered the scene as a young man in the heyday of Beaverbrook Newspapers and stayed in Fleet Street's Black Lubyanka for almost all his professional life.

His career provides the thread which binds the days of Beaverbrook with those of Beaverbrook's heirs, for he successfully rode the roller-coaster of the Express group's changing fortunes. Virtually impregnable in his position and well aware of his almost incalculable value to the paper, he survived and prospered as the group he worked for went through two traumatic changes of ownership. In 1978 the Beaverbrook family sold their birthright for a £13 million mess of pottage to Trafalgar House plc, and its managing director Victor Matthews took control. In 1985 David Stevens and United Newspapers bought control. In both cases, with very different men in charge, Junor managed to survive, showing the same obsequiousness and cunning which had served him so well with Beaverbrook.

By the time Lord ('Call me Clive') Hollick and his MAI group took power over the Express group newspapers' fortunes in 1996, Junor had gone and was spending his sunset years writing his JJ column for the *Express's* long-time deadly rival, Lord Rothermere's Associated Newspapers group and, in particular, for the *Mail on Sunday*, successful rival to the *Sunday Express* and a newspaper which Junor long maintained would never see the light of day. I would have loved to see him take on Hollick and his army of consultants and bean-counters. I know he would have put up a good fight and I suspect he would have survived.

For Junor was a master of newspaper office politics. He had the gift of shifting sides when it suited and raising obsequiousness to an art form. He bullied the unfortunate who were in no position to answer back with the enthusiasm of the playground sadist and treated women with calculated brutality.

When he died in 1997, at the reasonably ripe old age, at least for a Fleet Street editor, of 77, he received the traditional memorial service in St Bride's Church in Fleet Street, the 'parish church' of newspaper men and women. His peers bade their farewells in due fashion. On such occasions little ill, if any, is said of the dead. But at times during the service the oleaginous nature of some of the tributes was almost too much. Rarely had the famous JJ catchphrase, 'Pass the sickbag, Alice', seemed more appropriate. For the real Junor was a very different man from the one his readers might have thought they knew. Many who had cause to realise what he was really like simply stayed away. Hypocrisy sometimes has too high a price even for Fleet Street hacks.

There were no half measures with Junor. People either admired him or loathed him; and vice versa. What no one questioned was his professionalism as an editor, no matter how quirky, at times eccentric, his editing could be.

Above all, Junor was a living link with the birth of the paper itself, for he had been personally appointed by Lord Beaverbrook to the editorship of the paper which Beaverbrook had founded in 1919, and had been a trusted confidant of that magnificent and malevolent old despot.

Junor learned much at the feet of the press baron, and tried to resemble him in many ways, sharing not only his political views but also his autocratic style and his often cavalier attitude to women. He was a regular attendant at the Beaver's house parties at Cherkley Court, the 30-bedroomed Grade II listed Surrey estate where powerful politicians and beautiful women danced attendance, where plots were hatched and reputations shredded.

The Beaverbook ménage was meat and drink to Junor, then in his mid-thirties, and he revelled in the political intrigues and the games politicians played with one another, and with the unsuspecting voters. After all, he had by then fought and lost as a parliamentary Liberal candidate in the 1945 general election, and he rapidly realised that he could exercise a great deal more influence by rising to the top of his chosen profession and becoming an editor.

Junor would often tell listeners that after his parliamentary defeat the Beaver took him to one side and said that if his choice was to continue in politics, 'you will reach the highest echelons. But if it is journalism, I will put on your head a golden crown.'

A golden crown in the offing was worth more than a long climb up the political greasy pole and Junor chose the crown.

The Beaver secretly appointed Junor editor of the *Sunday Express* months before the then editor, Harold Keeble, who had succeeded the legendary John Gordon, learned of his fate. Such tactics did not make editors feel secure. Junor developed an ulcer, and champagne caused him agonies. But Beaverbrook had a tendency to write off anyone who had anything except the most trivial of illnesses, and he insisted on his guests drinking champagne (although the Beaver hated the stuff and drank whisky instead). All that summer, after he had been given the editorship, but before it had been announced, Junor drank champagne at Beaverbrook's table.

For some years, Junor had a 'grace and favour' house on Beaverbrook's Cherkley estate. This easy access to the 'ear' of the Old Man therefore gave Junor an advantage over his rivals in the group. Yet in some ways Junor paid a heavy price for living on the Cherkley estate and wearing his 'golden crown'. It meant that Junor was at the beck and call of the Beaver, who would call and demand urgent attention at any time of the day or night. Junor's family life suffered as a result.

Even when Junor first knew him, Beaverbrook's greatest days were behind him and the days when he could make or break governments were long gone. But he was still sole proprietor of two of Britain's greatest national newspapers, whose own dog-days lay in the future and whose voice still carried enormous authority.

At the time of Beaverbrook's death in 1964 both newspapers were selling in excess of four million copies daily; the only mass voice to the middle classes. Junor watched, learned and avidly digested the lessons he was learning, and in years to come was to relish the role he was to play as an acknowledged opinion maker, a man whom politicians, ministers and even Prime Ministers courted.

Although Junor came to dominate the *Sunday Express* over his 32 years, what is often forgotten is that he had several close calls during his career in the early days. When writing about alleged malfeasances by certain Labour MPs over petrol rationing during the 1956 Suez Canal crisis, he was held to have committed contempt of parliament and was forced to make an apology before the bar of the House of Commons, a very rare occurrence. During this period of uncertainty Beaverbrook let Junor swing slowly in the wind. Had Junor not put up a spirited defence and been let off by the House, then he would not have lasted as editor.

The second crisis came in 1963 when he fell out with Beaverbrook who was trying to persuade him to soften the tone of his leader pages. In particular, Beaverbrook was still supporting the Prime Minister, Harold Macmillan, with whom Junor was becoming increasingly disillusioned. Junor resigned on the grounds that while the proprietor had the absolute right to decide the paper's policies, as editor he would on grounds of conscience be unable to support Macmillan when the Prime Minister called a general election. Beaverbrook insisted that JJ work his notice and suggested he wrote articles during this period. Junor refused and said that he must either continue to edit the paper until the notice expired or be paid off.

The two men rarely spoke during this period and, indeed, rarely communicated. Junor was in effect sent to Coventry. Some weeks later, at the height of the Profumo crisis, Macmillan announced he was to have a prostate gland operation. Beaverbrook rang Junor: 'You are saved,' he said. 'He's bound to go and you can stay ...' Macmillan did in fact resign. Beaverbrook and Junor buried the hatchet and Junor stayed in the editor's chair for a further 23 years.

This then, was the Fleet Street giant with whom I was to work closely – and sometimes too closely – for eleven years. Those years left me with a great deal of respect for the man, but they didn't blind me to his many imperfections; and the closer you looked at the forbidding public face of John Junor, the more you became aware of the warts that often disfigured it.

I was thrown into the lion's den in 1978 after the Trafalgar House take-over when Victor Matthews started taking stock of the new acquisition. He found that the *Sunday Express* – the great newspaper whose £12 million a year profits were the 'milch cow' of the Express group – was being run as a sinecure by a 21-year-old whose qualifications for the job consisted almost entirely of his distinguished lineage. Maxwell Aitken, later the 3rd Baron Beaverbrook, was the youngest general manager in Fleet Street, a position which owed everything to the fact that he was Beaverbrook's grandson and the son of Sir Max Aitken, who had refused the peerage out of deference to his father.

But now the days of the Aitkens were gone, and Victor started looking urgently and rather desperately for someone who knew something about the *Sunday Express* business. I caught his eye. At that time I was an assistant general manager, and perhaps because I not only knew the *Sunday Express*, but was also indisputably not an Aitken, I was appointed to replace young Maxwell.

From this place at the right hand of Junor, I was in the perfect position to watch as he played his cards with the skill of a master bridge player – and sometimes he overplayed his hand with a fawning obsequiousness which was a long way from the almost lordly arrogance of his public persona.

I was in Victor's office one day when the intercom buzzed and the unmistakable voice of the laird of Auchtermuchty (the Scottish town which he frequently used in his column to illustrate his wide range of opinions and prejudices) boomed out of the phone's loudspeaker. 'What a wonderful party you gave last week, Victor,' he declared.

It was a shallow rather than a graceful compliment, for Victor well knew his own social limitations and gloomily recognised that his occasional parties were almost inevitably social disasters. As Junor waffled on, Victor's eyes twinkled and he put his hand to his mouth in a 'fingers down the throat' gesture which mimed his disgust at the editor's empty flattery.

Although Junor himself may have choked on his words, they were part of his game plan to keep his privileged position, and they undoubtedly worked. No matter what Victor may have thought 'off the record', he was very much aware of Junor's value to the paper and enjoyed having this legendary figure creep to him; and no doubt Junor's influence in high places ensured Victor's elevation to the peerage in due course.

But then Junor had a long history of knowing how to ingratiate himself with those in power. It had started a long time previously in the Beaver's days. One story is typical.

On one of Beaverbrook's birthdays, Junor decided to give the Old Man a present with a difference – a sheepdog whistle, the kind that is inaudible to the human ear. But, once purchased, Junor began to have second thoughts and became anxious.

'Do you think he'll get the joke?' he asked a colleague. 'You know, he's the shepherd, we're the sheep.'

A few days later a bemused Beaverbrook was overheard saying to a friend, 'Junor sent me a whistle that didn't blow.' He paused thoughtfully. 'The pea must have fallen out ...'

So far as I know, Junor never gave Victor a sheepdog whistle but he certainly let it be known that he was at his new master's service and that Victor only had to whistle.

So JJ continued to rule, and to enjoy the full range of perks and privileges of his almost royal status within Express Newspapers. His expenses used to come to me for approval, and for all practical purposes I might as well have had a rubber stamp for my signature. Junor always had a disdain amounting almost to contempt for mere managerial types, and one had to rise to board level before he would deign to treat the *Express* management as anything more than inky pen-pushers.

So his expenses were extensive and often largely anonymous. The column where those allegedly lunched were supposed to be identified was often filled with the bald statement 'contacts known to the chairman', though this would be as meaningless to the chairman as it was to me.

Every year, too, there was a golfing holiday in the Gambia, which would be followed in his column by flattering comments on that country and its president, a golfing companion. The costs were paid by the *Express* under a special 'overseas travel allowance' which gave Junor the freedom to travel to where he chose as part of his untaxed remuneration package.

Yet when it came to signing the expenses of his staff, Junor was every bit as tight-fisted as Scots are often portrayed. I recall him discussing with me the expenses of Bob McWilliams, who was then news editor. 'Andrew,' he said to me, 'for years McWilliams's expenses have been averaging three pounds ten shillings a week. Lately they have risen to three pounds fifteen shillings. Do you think he's keeping a mistress?' I laughed, but the smile died on my lips when I realised with astonishment that Junor was deadly serious.

Junor had a notoriously short attention span.

Ted Westropp, the amiable if long-winded City editor, once came in to see JJ with an interminable tale which even JJ found hard to interrupt. He idly picked up a pair of new binoculars he had bought for his yacht and held them up to his eyes. Westropp's flow began to falter. 'Amazing,' said Junor, 'I can see the pigeons shitting on the roof of St Bride's Church ...'

He also could also be high-handed. On the first day that a new young reporter called Perry arrived, Junor called him into his office. 'You have a wonderful opportunity ahead of you, Mr Perry. Play your cards right on the *Sunday Express* and I shall have your name up in lights. You can see it – "Don Perry, *Sunday Express* reporter".'

Perry's first name wasn't Don. In fact I doubt if anyone in the office knew his real name. But JJ had decided he was Don (knowing full well it wasn't) and Perry was too timid to correct the great man. So Perry's by-line appeared in the *Sunday Express* as 'Don Perry' for very many years and his by-line was to gain a certain immortality by appearing as 'Dom Perignon' in *Private Eye*. It was yet another sign of Junor flexing his power against those who couldn't fight back.

He would bully the weak and be vindictive to the strong once their powers had waned. A classic case was his relationship with John Gordon, his predecessor as editor of the *Sunday Express*.

John Gordon, in his lifetime, was as legendary a Scot as Junor and equally cantankerous. Not surprisingly, Junor had no time for John Gordon and Gordon had even less for Junor. As Gordon grew older his powers began to wane. For several years before he died, JJ ghosted the John Gordon column which was published under Gordon's name. Increasingly frail and lame, and finally having a leg amputated, Gordon still insisted on coming into the office from time to time until close to the end he had a special handrail built for him in the front foyer to help him climb the few stairs from the foyer to the lift. On John Gordon's death, Junor moved quickly to have this special handrail removed. The King is dead. Long live the King!

Private Eye was a magazine which JJ took great care to avoid appearing in, and he did so with his customary cunning. (He didn't relish the idea of his exploits, especially those of a sexual nature, being bandied about in that notorious organ.) In the magazine's early days in the 1960s, he had taken the precaution to befriend its brilliant, if eccentric editor, Richard Ingrams. They used to lunch fairly regularly, swapping political gossip. This did not mean that Junor escaped entirely Scot free. Ingrams once parodied a piece in the JJ column in which Junor had reminisced about an old colleague from his Fleet Air Arm days who he described as a 'white-haired boy in a Nissen hut near Deal'.

Variations on the piece appeared again and again in the *Eye*, inexplicably describing a 'white-haired boy in a Nissen hut near Deal' in the most inappropriate stories. Junor was utterly mystified by the joke, never realising that his mystification was itself the joke. Ingrams would almost weep with laughter at the thought of the elderly Scottish editor's puzzlement on reading another instalment of the tale of the Nissen hut-dwelling, white-haired boy of Deal.

Despite being stigmatised with the invisible label 'management' around my neck, I forged a working relationship with Junor, and on at least two occasions he defended me against the moods of Jocelyn Stevens, managing director of the group during most of the reign of Max Aitken and Victor Matthews. The mutual loathing between Junor and Stevens provides some of the most dramatic encounters in the history of the *Express* although most of the skulduggery occurred behind the arras.

Junor would sometimes play at management himself and maintained his own dialogue with the unions, entertaining chapel officials in his office late into the night with copious quantities of Famous Grouse whisky. Of course, the 'lads' were highly flattered by the attentions of the famous editor, and when drink had loosened his tongue Junor did not need much encouragement to deliver his scathing opinions of the quality of our management. The chapel officials had no hesitation in using these opinions when they next came to negotiate with us, and the whole exercise was distinctly counter-productive when it came to dancing with the print union wolves.

He also liked to play games with the management and would frequently ask me to dine with him on Saturday nights at the then Terrazza Est restaurant in Chancery Lane, where he had his own window seat. The purpose of these dinners appeared to be digging for dirt about my senior management colleagues, and the smallest shred of gossip would be carefully dropped by him into later conversations (which in turn damaged the reputation of those who were clearly his informants). But Junor's word games were already notorious, and I always tried to be especially careful about what I said when in the company of the illustrious editor.

I also came to realise that this fabled man had weaknesses, both as a man and as a journalist. Although his writings would lead you to believe he was a model of propriety inside the office, JJ had more than an eye for the women when he felt himself 'off parade'. At company functions he could make a nuisance of himself, and staff wives told me they found it quite an ordeal to attend office cricket matches with him as he made lecherous advances and, they said, attempted to grope them behind the pavilion.

So it was no surprise to me to learn that several women who worked on the *Sunday Express* had affairs with him and one writer claimed to have had a son by him. She later tried to pursue a paternity claim which named Junor as the father, but failed when blood tests didn't support her claim. It was said that the tests were 'fixed' by Junor's doctor, a personal friend, who switched his client's blood with that of an innocent patient.

Another who fell for his not obviously apparent charms was a young secretary who worked in the features department. It happened in 1979 when Junor celebrated not only his 60th birthday, but also his 25th year as editor of the *Sunday Express*, and the staff held a lunch in his honour which was attended by, among many others, Prime Minister Margaret Thatcher and Lord Hailsham.

It was a good lunch, and like many good lunches it went on and on and on. Junor stayed all afternoon and got completely pickled – the only time I ever saw him in such a state – and by 6 p.m. he was fumbling at the dresses of almost every woman in sight, and inviting them to return with him to his home near Dorking.

The secretary, in her mid-twenties and in awe of the great man, accepted his invitation. They returned first to Fleet Street, where Junor pounced on her in his office. But they were interrupted in mid-thrust by the sports editor Les Vanter, who wanted to show Junor a page proof, though it was immediately obvious to him that there was only one kind of sport on his editor's mind.

Junor and his young prize then caught the Dorking train from Waterloo but by the time the train reached Clapham Junction, his bladder was at bursting point – and he was trapped in a train without a corridor or on-board toilet. Unable to contain himself any further, the man who regularly scourged both drunken yobbos and British Rail threw open the carriage door and peed on the track.

Eventually the couple reached JJ's house, and the secretary spent the night in Junor's bed. But although the editor's spirit may have been willing, the spirits he had drunk enforced their familiar form of birth control and sexual activity was by then out of the question.

However, the next morning Junor was ready at least to talk a good fight, and he told the girl he would make her Lady Junor (ignoring the point that the role was already filled) and wanted to 'make babies' with her.

So began a six-week affair, with most of the action taking place on Friday nights in the *Sunday Express* flat in Clarges Street where JJ would insist on watching his favourite TV show, *I Love Lucy*, before getting down to the main event. The old rogue must have had unsuspected talents and/or charms, for the girl fell desperately in love with him and seriously believed that he wanted to marry her – she was utterly devastated when Junor told her that he could not continue the relationship.

Perhaps by then Junor had his eye on an even bigger catch – the glamorous TV star Selina Scott, whom he claimed to have 'discovered' and on whom he was fixated almost to the point of obsession. He frequently wrote glowing words about her in his column and in his book *Listening for a Midnight Tram* fulsomely describes her as 'gorgeous, delightful warm, compassionate and unaffected'.

Whether JJ had his way with Selina is not clear, though he liked it to be thought that he had.

One day in the spring of 1980 he arrived in the office in such an uncharacteristically good mood that his staff were curious about his dreamy, amiable state of mind. Over lunch with colleagues he explained that the night before he had shared dinner with Selina, and strongly implied that the entertainment involved a good deal more than dinner. And later that day, the foreign editor, Peter Vane, went into his office and caught him penning a letter which started 'Selina Darling ...'

Later that year Selina was his personal guest at the traditional Boat Show lunch then organised by Express Newspapers and there seemed little doubt in the minds of those present that JJ saw himself and Selina as an 'item'. I think not, or only in his dreams; if only because of Junor's own description of her as 'a shrewd observer ... 100 per cent her own woman and utterly incorruptible'.

Certainly Junor enjoyed success elsewhere. The literary agent George Greenfield once said that he and JJ went to Germany together to tie up a book deal for the *Sunday Express* and on the second night of their two-day visit Junor unexpectedly disappeared. The following morning Greenfield turned up at the airport for the return flight – to find his companion unashamedly smooching in the departure lounge with an extremely attractive German woman. He never found out who she was.

Although he was undeniably a great editor, John Junor was also flawed as a journalist. He often seemed to shy away from major hard news stories, instead preferring the role of behind-the-scenes wheeler-dealer.

As an example of this approach, Junor himself tells the story in his book of how in the early 1980s he was tipped off that Maurice Oldfield, former head of MI6 and then called out of retirement by Margaret Thatcher to head security in Northern Ireland, was a practising and promiscuous homosexual. The source was impeccable – none other than the Metropolitan Police Commissioner himself, David McNee, who also clearly indicated to Junor that the hall porter in the block of flats where Oldfield lived would 'sing like a bird' if asked about the heavy traffic in young male visitors to the Oldfield flat.

McNee had already tipped off the Cabinet Secretary about the situation in the hope that he would pass on the word to the Prime Minister. But Oldfield was Thatcher's own appointment, and McNee feared that no one would pluck up the courage to tell the Prime

Minister that her chosen man was himself a security risk. Would Junor help?

Of course he would. Junor immediately set up lunch with Mrs Thatcher's personal private secretary and enlisted her help in getting a letter to the Iron Lady without anybody else – especially the No. 10 staff – seeing it. Junor wrote the letter which blew the gaff on Oldfield, and the private secretary ensured that it lay unopened on Mrs Thatcher's bed for her eyes only.

A few weeks later it was quietly announced that Oldfield would not be completing his tour of duty in Ulster, and no doubt Junor congratulated himself on a job well done and a successful bit of sycophancy.

But at no time, it appears, did he consider what would have been second nature to most journalists; to send a reporter to the garrulous hall porter, standing up the story, and printing an exclusive which would have the rest of Fleet Street chasing round in circles in an effort to catch up with what should have been a tremendous *Sunday Express* 'splash'.

There were many other episodes which showed his weakness in judging hard news. Instead he would issue what his staff called 'pronouncements' – dogmatic statements which instantly acquired the status of having been carved in granite and from which he would never retreat despite all evidence to the contrary. These included statements such as his regular assertion throughout the 1980s: 'Mark my words, Ronald Reagan will be dead within six months', uttered in such portentous tones that the listeners were led to believe that Junor had inside knowledge from the White House and the President's own doctors.

He also came up with stories which everyone else missed, largely because no story existed. For example, on New Year's Eve 1985, Junor was standing in the garden of his Surrey home when he heard a loud bang 'some miles to the north' which he decided was an IRA bomb.

Next morning there was no mention of the bomb on the radio news, and Junor ordered the news desk to carry out a major investigation into what he called 'this extraordinary cover-up'. In a very short time reporters had cleared up the non-mystery. New Year revellers had let off thunderflashes in a garden a few miles north of Junor's garden at exactly the same time as Junor's 'bomb', and the reports were so loud that angry neighbours called the police.

But this mundane explanation did not satisfy the editor. He accused his chief reporter, Michael Dove, of being 'naive' in accepting it, and insisted on further investigations. These lasted another three days, and of course yielded nothing. No doubt Junor believed there was a cover-up over the Surrey 'bomb' to his dying day.

Anyone who has seen Humphrey Bogart as Captain Queeg in the film *The Caine Mutiny* will recognise something of Junor in Queeg's obsession with the missing tin of strawberries.

On the other hand there was no doubt that Junor was himself a target when he was pursued down the A3 on two successive weekends by menacing-looking chaps in unmarked cars, and on one occasion escaped only by driving his Lotus Elite into Dorking police station.

There were understandable fears that he was being set up by the IRA, but the truth may be a little simpler – Junor had clashed with two over-officious coppers from the City of London force who had accused him of turning the wrong way into Fleet Street.

JJ was infuriated by the heavy-handed coppers and not only made a formal complaint to the City of London Police Commissioner but also pilloried the policemen in his column. In fact, he made such a fuss that his friend David McNee, the Metropolitan Police Commissioner, reckoned the most likely explanation of the weekend car chase was simply the errant PC Plods, or their colleagues, setting out to put the frighteners on JJ.

But Junor, ever a good man for a juicy conspiracy theory, concluded that it was all part of the same plot when his son Roderick was found slumped on the pavement near Waterloo Station. He made it plain he believed Roderick had been the victim of a vicious attack, either by the IRA or by more vengeful coppers. The truth was laughably simple – Roderick had fallen over in a stupor that owed everything to strong drink and nothing either to strong coppers or strong IRA hit men.

Junor was also surprisingly naive in other ways, and sometimes fell for the most outlandish stories. For instance, there was a woman reader who wrote to him from the Isle of Wight to inform him that her husband, who had died seven years previously, had returned to her and was living in her bedroom – disguised as a red admiral butterfly. She knew for certain it was her husband and the proof was there for all to see; the butterfly had a torn wing which exactly matched an arm injury her late husband had once suffered.

Preposterous? Of course – but JJ took the sad lady's story so seriously that he insisted a reporter be sent to the Isle of Wight to investigate. The bewildered reporter, presumably wondering whether this was the sort of thing he had spent his career to achieve, duly reported that not only was there no husband, but he couldn't even see a Red Admiral butterfly. None of which stopped Junor from unmercifully haranguing the news desk for failing to stand up the utterly ludicrous story.

Junor was a strange mixture of apparent concern for others and malevolence. Staff often told of individual acts of kindness. But, towards his staff, such gestures often seemed to smack of the lord of the manor showing a certain generosity to his serfs. Indeed, as I have shown, when it came to his female retainers, Junor believed strongly in the *droit de seigneur*.

He was basically a bully who would withdraw quickly if challenged strongly. His obsequiousness to those in authority was characteristic of his type. I could not but admire his ability to survive both proprietors and ever-changing editors of the sister *Daily Express*, whom he did his best to undermine (only a few like Larry Lamb did he steer clear of tackling). But he was allowed to cling to power too long and as a result this led to the decline of the paper that, at his prime, he had done so much to create.

And he always knew best. One story is typical. In 1981 the then general manager informed him, on best advice, that Associated Newspapers were certainly going to go ahead with the launch of the *Mail on Sunday*. Junor was scornful. 'You have been listening to too much tittle-tattle in El Vino's. Let me tell you this – there will never be a *Mail on Sunday* – never!'

Today, the *Mail on Sunday* is selling well over two million while the *Sunday Express* struggles to hold one million; and, of course, Junor spent his declining years writing his JJ column for the *Mail on Sunday*.

10

AFTER JUNOR
The Kiss of Death

EVEN JOHN JUNOR recognised that he could not continue as editor of the *Sunday Express* indefinitely, though his health remained as robust as his views. But the date and manner of his going were very much of his choosing; he had let it be known that he would be prepared to hand over the reins in 1986 when he had completed 32 years in the chair. So far as the readers were concerned, however, the plan was to ensure that they would barely see the join between editors. All the decision takers involved agreed that while changes were necessary, nothing radical (such as going tabloid) was on the cards. Above all, Junor was to continue writing the JJ column which was such an integral part of the paper.

So David Stevens went shopping for a man to replace the irreplaceable, a man who could follow the legendary Junor, take the *Sunday Express* in a different direction, yet retain all the existing readers and still operate under the brooding eye of the man who would also be the paper's star columnist. It was a nigh-impossible task. Stevens did not consult Junor about his successor, although he did keep him informed about the candidates he was considering.

Eventually Stevens came up with what was widely recognised as a safe choice – Robin Esser, who was then features editor of the *Daily Express* and a former northern editor of the paper. The appointment met with Junor's guarded approval, for as he later wrote: 'If I had been antagonistic to the final choice of Robin Esser, I would have left the paper there and then.'

Junor did not leave the paper although he left the building. The old editor became a sort of king in exile, for he was given an office in the Tudor Street headquarters of United Newspapers, which he described as 'a cathedral of calm and tranquillity' after the frenetic activity of the Fleet Street offices just a few hundred yards away. The move also gave the old and new editors their own territories although JJ's weekly column remained very much off-limits to Esser and it was clearly understood that he touched the Junor column at his peril.

To his credit, this was never a problem for Esser, for he knew full well that he needed all the help he could get in his faltering paper's constant circulation battle with the *Mail on Sunday*, and the JJ column was very much a plus point. So the old and new editors worked in harness well enough, although it soon became all too apparent that the safe choice of Esser was perhaps too safe. Esser didn't rock any boats, he got on reasonably well with Junor, but he did not give the paper anything it did not have before.

True, following Junor would have been a formidable task for any top journalist. He had held power and stamped his personality on the *Sunday Express* for so long that anyone accepting the position knew he was being offered a poisoned chalice.

Indeed, many a talented journalist held back, knowing instinctively that, although for a period the new editor would enjoy the trappings of power, the man to succeed Junor would find his days were numbered from the very first time he stepped into the stark office on the fifth floor that had been Junor's eyrie for so long and sat in the *Sunday Express* editor's chair.

The pub pundits of Fleet Street thought that the editor who would inevitably follow Junor's immediate successor would stand a better chance. The general consensus was that the first post-Junor editorship would begin the process of de-Junorisation in the same way that in the

Soviet Union Khrushchev had begun the process of de-Stalinisation while Khrushchev's successor, Brezhnev, completed it. (The comparisons should not be taken too seriously, of course, but it was indicative of Junor's long hold on power!)

Esser was an expert at 'managing upwards', and his colleagues during his varied career never felt they could quite trust him. As a young journalist on the *Express* his contemporary, and rival, was David English – later Sir David English – editor of the *Daily Mail*, whose circulation over the years rose as surely as that of its once much more successful competitor, the *Daily Express*, fell.

Esser, who had a spell with Associated Newspapers, returned to the *Express* at the invitation of Christopher Ward to produce a new weekend feature supplement. There he shared a narrow, grim room, albeit on the executive floor, its large heating pipes crawling all over the ceiling, with Leith McGrandle, a former city editor of the *Evening Standard*, who shortly afterwards went on to become deputy editor of the *Daily Express*. They were known as the 'Boiler Room Boys'. Several years later Esser was to join McGrandle as features editor on the *Express* under the editorship of Larry Lamb. The 'Boiler Room Boys' had made it.

Esser made some of the usual changes of a new editor. New layouts and columns were introduced. But the changes were cosmetic and I couldn't help feeling that his heart wasn't really in the job. Esser had been an ambitious man but by the time he reached the top a lot of the fizz had gone.

Esser may have started with vaulting ambitions and dreams of greatness, but if he had them he did not impose them on the paper. It is perhaps a sad but fitting commentary on his stewardship that he started as caretaker editor of the *Sunday Express* and finished in the same role.

Yet in one respect he was very much the equal of Junor and that, almost inevitably, was in his private life. This dated from Robin's Manchester days as northern editor of the *Daily Express*.

The object of his desires was a vivacious, and voracious, lady named Tui France, then the northern classified manager of the *Express*. Their relationship had long been an open secret in the Manchester office.

Tui was a highly attractive woman who positively exuded sex appeal and dynamism, and she and Esser embarked on a lengthy and high-tension affair. But she was initially thwarted in her clear ambition to snare and marry Esser, for after the tragedy of his first wife's death, Esser rebounded not into Tui's arms but into those of a delightful lady who immediately filled the now vacant role of mother to his young children. I watched her with the children one day at the City Golf Club; she obviously cared deeply for them, and Robin soon married her. But although Esser was now London-based, so was Tui – she had moved to HQ and she was perhaps not at all pleased that the man with whom she was besotted had married someone else.

Eventually, a divorce took place and Tui married her Robin. During his tenure as *Sunday Express* editor, she gained quite a reputation as a socialite. Tui was deeply ambitious on Esser's behalf. I suspect that she suffered more from Esser's inevitable departure from the editor's chair than even he did.

In due course, and in true Fleet Street tradition, it was felt by a basically incompetent board that since the *Sunday Express* was making no great progress in the war with the *Mail on Sunday*, a scapegoat should be found.

The answer was to appoint a new editor who would lead the *Sunday Express* to nirvana. An idea to appoint an acting editor while Esser was sent abroad on an extended sabbatical was rightly rejected by Stevens as 'underhand'.

Robin Esser's response to his dismissal, with suitable compensation, was one of shock and horror. 'Mrs Thatcher isn't going to like this,' he warned.

A week later, I bumped into Mrs T. at a function. She said to me, 'Nice man, Robin Esser. May I ask, who is the next editor?'

The answer was Robin Morgan. He was to prove a disaster for the *Sunday Express*.

11

MORGAN
Who He?

FOLLOWING THE DEPARTURE of Esser from the *Sunday Express* and his replacement by Robin Morgan, John Junor did not hang around for long. Morgan proved to be an editor too far for Junor, who was especially upset by an interview which Morgan had given very soon after his appointment in which he proceed to pour a bucket of the brown stuff on the *Sunday Express* as he had found it, with particularly unkind references to the Junor decades. Junor, having collected as much money as he could from the Express Group, promptly did a deal with his, and our, old arch-enemy Lord Rothermere. Junor eagerly took the good lord's shilling (in his case closer to £100,000 for one JJ column a week).

The *Mail on Sunday* was justifiably cock-a-hoop at the Junor coup, but their joy would have been unconfined had they known the calibre of the man who was now shakily guiding the *Sunday Express* ship from the editor's bridge. Robin Morgan was a mistake and a bad one. He brought nothing to the paper of any consequence apart from some meaningless fiddling with design and typography, and he was viewed with scorn bordering on contempt by those of his staff whom he had not appointed. He had originally applied for the job as editor of the *Yorkshire Post* and was seen by Gordon Linacre who had shown, with his approval of Roger Boase, for example, that he was no great shakes as a judge of men. He was impressed by the superficially charming Morgan who talked a great book about himself. Linacre convinced Stevens that Morgan would make a good editor of the *Sunday Express* and Stevens, not for the first time, bowed to Linacre's advice on editorial matters.

Morgan was a prime example of someone being promoted not one notch above their ability but half a dozen. His ignorance of some of the basics of newspapers was frightening. I remember him telling me one day that he was going to eliminate 'cross-heads' from the newspaper, which he felt were 'old fashioned'. If he had been allowed to do this the paper would have been filled with great slabs of unreadable type. Fortunately, I prevented him from carrying out this instruction to his sub-editors just in time.

His grip on news stories was even more erratic than Junor's or Esser's, perhaps best shown by the story he printed about Cypriots fleeing from one side to the other of that partitioned island. For the story was illustrated by a large picture of refugees apparently caught in the act of fighting their way through a fierce roll of barbed wire. In fact the barbed wire had been set up on an English beach, and the picture was a fake. But in Morgan's view of newspaper ethics, it was a perfectly acceptable subterfuge, because the picture showed how it 'might' have looked in real life.

However, in one respect at least, if indeed the only one, Morgan followed in the well-worn footsteps of Junor and Esser and that was in his relationships with women. For he, too, apparently considered himself God's gift to women despite looking to my jaundiced eye more like the school swot than a Lothario. Several times he was reported to me for making crude and suggestive remarks to female members of his staff, and there were complaints about his fumbled verbal gropings. 'Want to go out with a big boy?' was his none-too-subtle approach, the leer on his face magnified by his Hank Marvin heavy-framed spectacles. Had I known then what I know now, Robin Morgan's tenure of office at the *Sunday Express* would have been even shorter.

The *Marchioness*, a pleasure boat full of young people on a disco fun trip up the Thames, was run down by the bulk carrier *Bow Bell* on the night of 20 August 1990 and overturned immediately with much loss of life. Passengers were drowned in the cold waters of the fast-flowing river, and any onlookers were powerless to help. It is one of the many scandals of the disaster that the Thames, London's major artery to the sea, had no river-based emergency rescue service to deal with events such as this.

The disaster happened at 11.20 p.m. on a Saturday night, and the boat went down within sight of the *Express* offices, between Blackfriars and Southwark bridges. It was long after the first-edition deadlines for all the Sunday newspapers, but the *Sunday Express* was virtually on the spot and ideally placed to deliver the first and best coverage of one of the biggest news stories of the year. And, because of the time the accident happened, it was also one of the few occasions for a newspaper to steal a march on the electronic news media.

But where was the editor of the *Sunday Express*? Who was going to lead the *Express* journalists into action? The editor of a Sunday newspaper – indeed, any newspaper – should never leave the building until his/her paper is printing, should return to organise and supervise the changes for later editions, and should be contactable at all times until the last copy of the last edition is printed to deal with 'breaking stories' just like the *Marchioness* disaster.

But on the night the *Marchioness* sank, Robin Morgan was nowhere to be found. He had not left a contact number with the news desk, and even his deputy editor, Charles Garside, had no idea where he was. Perhaps, he had gone home? No, there was no response to the frantic telephone calls to his home from the office.

So where was he? Apparently not on *Sunday Express* business. For on this night of all nights, and as the *Marchioness* went down, the editor was lost somewhere – but where?

Thus it was left to the deputy to fill the editor's role, and a splendid job he made of it. Garside commandeered and designed new pages, organised the rudderless journalists, ordered extra copies of the paper to be printed, and produced a paper which suffered not at all by comparison with its rivals next day, nor by the absence of its editor.

In fact, Morgan seemed totally unaware of the frenetic activity in his absence, for when he was telephoned on Sunday morning and was asked what he thought of his paper's coverage of the disaster, it was not clear if he had yet seen the *Sunday Express*. Imagine – a story of that magnitude and the editor had not bothered to find out how his paper had performed in his absence unless, of course, he still did not even know there had been a disaster.

But the full story of Morgan's absence on the night of the *Marchioness* did not emerge until much later, for his staff covered up for him in the immediate aftermath of the tragedy. So I was unaware of the full story at the time, which was fortunate for Morgan, for if I had known, I would have sacked him on the spot.

As for Charles Garside, the unsung hero of the hour who had rescued the *Sunday Express* from the wreckage of the *Marchioness*? I'm afraid that he never reaped the *Express* reward he deserved, for he was ignored when the time came to replace Morgan though I am pleased for him that he finally got an editorship for he went on to run and edit *The European*.

Following the Morgan fiasco, the *Sunday Express* was placed in the safe hands of Brian Hitchen, editor of the *Daily Star*, a patriotic professional, who quickly eradicated the detritus which had been Morgan's contribution to a great national newspaper.

Morgan swiftly returned to the journalistic obscurity from which he had been briefly plucked.

12

CHRISTOPHER WARD
A Talented Dreamer

CHRISTOPHER WARD'S first day as editor of the *Daily Express* was not auspicious. A keen gun sportsman, he turned up at the *Daily Express* building carrying a small case containing two hand guns.

The guard at the entrance to the building stopped him and asked him to open his case (it was at the height of one of the periodic IRA terrorist scares). Ward duly opened the bag, the guard took one look, whereupon he became apoplectic.

'Right, I'm calling the police right away!' he bellowed and reached for the telephone on the front desk.

'But I'm the new editor of the *Daily Express*!' Ward exclaimed.

'Editors of the *Daily Express* don't go around carrying guns,' replied the guard, an *Express* trusty of many years. 'But it's true!' Ward wailed. 'I *am* the editor of the *Daily Express*.'

The guard continued dialling the local Snow Hill police station.

Ward took direct action. He snatched the receiver, thrust it into the guard's face and bellowed, 'Phone Jocelyn – or you'll find your job's on the line.'

The guard, taken aback by this threat from a possible terrorist who claimed to be the editor of the *Daily Express*, took the receiver and gingerly phoned Jocelyn's office whereupon it was confirmed that the gunman in the entrance hall below was indeed the new editor. Jocelyn thought it was a huge joke, but all the same he insisted that Ward kept his guns in his safe at all times.

Ward had taken over at the beginning of the 1980s from the amiable giant Arthur Firth, an *Express* man of the old school, whose views were thought to be too 'Old *Express*' to carry the paper forward into the next decade. Firth in his time had replaced Derek Jameson, the Cockney sparrow who in his time ended up as editor of both the *Daily Express* and the *Daily Star*. Jameson, for his part, had taken over from Roy Wright, a former deputy editor of the *Evening Standard*, a belt-and-braces type of journalist.

Wright had succeeded the cerebral Alastair Burnett, a talented charmer whose strengths really lay in the editor's chair of the *Economist*, which he had filled with distinction for years before being enticed to the *Express*, or in a television studio as a distinguished 'front' man. The editorial floor of a middle-market newspaper was not his scene.

But this capricious pattern of filling the *Daily Express* editor's chair indicated the desperation with which the *Express* management tried to seek the editorial Holy Grail. First, someone different with fizz (Burnett), followed by a steady pair of hands (Wright) succeeded by a fizzy character again (Jameson) who, in due course, was replaced by another steady pair of hands (Firth).

Now it was time for some fizz again. Victor had been convinced that what the *Express* needed was a 'breath of young, fresh air', not least by Felicity Green, number four on the paper and a long-term mentor of Christopher Ward at the *Mirror* where they had both spent many years.

Ward had considerable charm and a good sense of humour. At the *Mirror* he had made his name as a witty writer and a good ideas man, especially in the features department. But there was a fey quality about him and he had the attention span of the proverbial gnat. He was just not cut out to be an editor of a national newspaper. While full of good ideas, he had little understanding of, or interest in, how a newspaper worked, especially the importance of news.

He was editor during the Falklands War. Here was a theme to appeal to all that the *Express* stood for – or used to. Ward came from reliable stock, his father also having been an *Express* man. But Ward had been too long at the *Mirror* and some of its pacific nature had entered his soul.

While the *Express* coverage of the Falklands War was good, it lacked the 'Heart of Oak' patriotism, the jingoism of the Old *Express* and which even New *Express* readers wanted to read in their newspaper. Ward's heart was never in it. Most days his resolve had to be stiffened and the news coverage hardened up by the older *Express* men who complained privately that Beaverbrook must be turning in his grave.

There was the inevitable fresh layout from a new editor. The Ward version was specially designed by an outside expert who favoured a box-type layout and insisted that stories be written, or cut, to fit into his pretty page designs. The old hands groaned. They had seen it all before. They shrugged their shoulders, kept their heads down and bided their time. After all, another editor would be along before too long.

But it was not Ward's news coverage or layouts which were to bring him down. It was his lack of control of budgets. Most editors are pretty hopeless with budgets but Ward was more hopeless than most. Like most new editors, he was given a relatively free hand for the first few months of his editorship but then was reined in. At this inevitable stage in the management–editor relationship, most editors scream and shout and then reach a *modus vivendi* with the management. Ward screamed and shouted and went on screaming and shouting while spending money freely if not always wisely.

This led him into a daily battle with management, most notably in the form of the general manager of the *Daily Express*, Tony 'Stonewall' Bentley, who had joined the company as a lad of sixteen in the circulation department and worked his way up the management ladder largely through saying 'no' to any editorial demand. Hence his nickname.

The rows between the two were famous. Day after day the trench warfare went on. I felt at the time that Ward was spending more time squabbling with Bentley than editing the paper. On top of the fact that the circulation continued to slide, the bad blood between the two was doing the paper no good.

Victor grew tired of the rows. Out of the blue – or rather Australia – the legendary Sir Larry Lamb, founding editor of the Murdoch *Sun*, had written to Victor 'offering his services'.

With Sir Larry's letter in his pocket, Victor felt that the time had come to sack Ward. Unfortunately, at that time Ward had just landed in California on a flight from Heathrow as part of the perk by which the *Express* editor could visit the States every year to check up on his American correspondents. Once a powerful force of twenty, the US staff had been reduced to three, but the perk continued.

Still jet-lagged from the east–west journey, Ward was ordered to return to London immediately and report to the chairman. Fearing the worst, Ward reluctantly boarded a plane straight back to Heathrow.

On arrival he was driven straight to Victor's office, not at the *Express*, but at the Trafalgar House headquarters off Piccadilly where Victor gently but firmly said his time had come to go the way of all previous *Express* editors.

Showing him the door, literally, Ward and Victor passed a model of the RMS *Titanic* which had been owned by the White Star Line, a predecessor of Cunard which had become a subsidiary of Trafalgar House.

Ward turned to Victor. 'You know, Victor, one of my relations was in the orchestra on the *Titanic* and he went down with the ship.'

Victor shook his head sadly and said, 'Life's tough, isn't it?'

The following day Ward took his numbers two and three out to lunch at the Savoy Grill. While still in a state of shock and jet-lag, in a way he seemed relieved. 'Well,' he said, 'at least I won't have to put up with Bentley's halitosis any longer.' There was only one thing he wanted on the menu – rack of lamb.

Ward later went on to co-found Redwood, the contract magazine publishing company, and become a millionaire.

So, in a way, he had the last laugh.

13

SIR LARRY LAMB
A Giant in his Day

SIR LARRY LAMB, editor of the *Daily Express* from 1983–6 was a big man in every way. Well over six foot, this cricket-loving Yorkshireman brought to the paper a distinguished past and a forbidding presence. His reputation had been made as the founding editor of Rupert Murdoch's *Sun* which he started from scratch in 1969. A former *Daily Mirror* man, he hastily assembled a group of hacks, some of whom had appeared ready for the knacker's yard, and inspired them into producing the most successful tabloid newspaper of the late twentieth century.

Sir Larry had inherited IPC's *Sun* , formerly the *Daily Herald*, the Labour Party broadsheet, which the veteran editor Lord Cudlipp had tried to relaunch as the newspaper for the age 'we live in'. Its combination of high-mindedness and Socialism was a flop and it was dying on its feet when Murdoch took over. Larry's team transformed the paper into the 'Soaraway *Sun*' and lifted the circulation from 650,000 to a firm 1,000,000 copies in its first 100 days. Within eight years Murdoch's *Sun* was selling over four million copies a day and had ousted the *Daily Mirror* as Britain's biggest-selling daily newspaper.

Sir Larry, a proud and stubborn man, had finally fallen out with his mentor Murdoch, but who still remained a very good friend, and gone off to Australia to work for Robert Holmes à Court, who was in the Isthmian League of newspaper proprietorship compared with Murdoch's Premier Division status. Sir Larry, whose knighthood was not unconnected with *The Sun*'s switch from being faintly pro-Labour to strongly pro-Mrs Thatcher before the 1979 general election, rapidly grew bored and wrote to Victor Matthews 'offering his services'. The timing was right. Victor, growing disillusioned with the editorship of Christopher Ward, jumped at the chance and Sir Larry took over the helm of the floundering *Daily Express*.

His first act, a wise one, was to keep in place as his deputy editor and second-in-command the recently installed and much younger man, Leith McGrandle, a former financial editor who, unusually for a journalist, had had experience in senior management (he was one of my successors as general manager of the *Sunday Express*). McGrandle, with his experience both in journalism and newspaper management, was invariably able to smooth over the inevitable tensions between an editor like Sir Larry, who always wanted to get his own way, and Victor and the management.

Sir Larry was one of the most talented editors of his generation but by the time he reached the *Daily Express* his greatest days were behind him. Yet he still brought a sense of leadership and direction which had been too often lacking in the past. And he had a natural instinct for a good news story. He left the day-to-day running of the paper to McGrandle although he usually insisted in drawing up the front page himself, using a pencil to sketch out the headlines and designs on the pad.

He brought not only a formidable reputation as an editor but as a 'bon viveur' and a lover of the good life in which he encouraged others to join in. During his time at *The Sun* there was an occasion when Murdoch had missed his flight to New York and unexpectedly returned to *The Sun*'s offices only to discover his senior staff 'discussing' the events of the day over whiskies in exceptionally large glasses.

He stormed into Sir Larry's office and roared, 'Let them drink my whisky if they must but must they drink it out of bloody plant pots?'

Larry was a fiercely loyal man and fought like a lion for those he believed in. Part of his strength was his happy family life, for throughout his career he was strongly supported by his charming wife Joan, also from Yorkshire, and he was intensely proud of his two sons and two daughters. A tall, good-looking man, Larry was very attractive to women but even if he had ever wanted to stray he would have found it difficult, for Joan guarded him like a lioness and was more in evidence at official functions than any editor's wife I knew.

Larry, while at the *Daily Express*, was still living on the reputation made as the first, and most successful, editor of the Murdoch *Sun* newspaper – famed in the industry as a chain-smoking, hard-drinking man's man who would have no truck with inferior journalistic standards. Frequently Larry would phone me late at night, getting me out of bed and complaining vigorously about the incompetence of the overpaid printworkers who were destroying his newspaper. On such occasions Larry was usually 'tired and emotional', as *Private Eye* would put it.

His expenses were a constant source of concern for me, especially as his taste for Burgundy was limited to the finest vintages. Looking at the wine list he would ask his guest, 'Would you like an experience or something ordinary?' Inevitably the guest would choose the 'experience' and the company would end up paying the bill for some of the finest contents of the restaurant's wine cellar.

Larry had some initial success. The in-paper Bingo craze, which added millions to newspaper circulations in the mid-1980s, rubbed off on the *Express* and was developed into the *Express* 'Millionaire's Club', a card game designed to produce the first 'reader millionaire'. For a time, the game added hundreds of thousands to the *Express* circulation and restored some of its former glory to the paper – at least in circulation terms. The odds were heavily stacked against there ever being a 'reader millionaire', although eventually we did have a winner – a man of such a doubtful past and reputation that we had to whisk him quickly out of the public eye, and our pages, so we never gained from the hoped-for publicity.

The whole newspaper Bingo craze of the 1980s finally petered out after a few disasters when misprinted cards led to thousands of readers claiming their prizes. The most notable was the day when the offices of our rivals, the *Daily Mail*, were besieged by hundreds of readers claiming their prizes (one disappointed couple stopped off at the *Daily Mail* offices on the way to Heathrow en route for their honeymoon). We rather enjoyed the *Daily Mail's* embarrassment but recognised that it could just as easily have happened to us.

Sir Larry also encouraged investigative journalism and had a number of 'scoops' which are the real meat and drink to newspapermen. Early in his editorship some of his team had discovered that there were faults in the intoxemeter which the police were using to breath-test potential drunk drivers. Innocent drivers, it was alleged, were being found guilty, even jailed, because of faulty equipment, The *Express* had the story chapter and verse, but Sir Larry, knowing it was a potentially explosive issue, phoned the then Home Secretary, Leon Brittan, to tell him what we were about to print.

The Home Secretary stalled but within an hour or so Larry was informed that a legal officer armed with a court order was on his way from Wales, where the makers of the intoxemeter were based, to stop the printing of the story. Since the story was already covering the front and centre pages and the deadline for printing was approaching, this posed a problem. Larry turned it to his advantage by printing the non-legally contentious parts of the story and deliberately leaving most of the centre pages empty on the basis that the *Express* had been forbidden by the law to reveal the 'truth' about the story. He eventually was allowed to publish and changes to the intoxemeter equipment were discreetly made.

Another scoop involved the tampering of petrol pumps with an electronic device which altered the reading on the petrol pump meter (in the customer's favour). This was of special interest to the head of our in-house legal department, who also owned a small filling station in the country, and had long wondered why his petrol takings never tallied with his fuel supplies (not in his favour!)

One 'scoop' which didn't come off involved a 'spoofish' front page at the height of the miners' strike attacking Arthur Scargill, the coal miners' union leader. The print unions, egged on by the National Union of Mineworkers, took exception and stopped the presses. We lost a whole day's production. Enormous pressure was put on Victor by the unions to get a 'right of reply'. Sir Larry was adamant. 'There is no right of reply in my newspaper,' he stormed, 'only a possible opportunity to reply at the editor's discretion.'

Victor, caught between the issue of editorial freedom and the company bank balance, was in a quandary. He wanted to settle the matter but Sir Larry refused to meet Victor unless the chairman personally requested that the editor went to see him. Not for the first time, McGrandle smoothed the way. He telephoned Mike Murphy, the then managing director and said, 'If you can get your man to phone my man to ask my man to come up and see your man I think we can settle the matter.' Victor gracefully complied. Larry stalked out of his office, turning only to say to McGrandle, un-Captain-Oates-like, 'I may not be some time.' He was some time. The 'possible right of reply' was given and the crisis was over. But ever since that day Sir Larry kept a green hold-all beneath his desk 'for the day I may have to leave'.

This crisis proved to be the only time that Victor was really painful to me. I was the humble number three in the management hierarchy and I happened to be in charge on the night of the 'possible right of reply'. When the miners responded with their reply, demanding it be printed verbatim, it proved to be an unprintable torrent of vitriol and abuse. Stalemate resulted.

I phoned Victor at home at 10.30 p.m. 'Sorry to bother you at home, chairman, but the men won't work, they have been leant on by the miners and are out again in sympathy.' 'Alright, Andrew,' said Victor. 'Keep me informed.'

At 12.30 I phoned again. 'Sorry, chairman, the presses are not running; I've met the men, cajoled them, threatened them and tried every trick but they won't move.'

' OK Andrew,' he replied.

I picked up the phone for the third time at 1.30 a.m. and had hardly uttered a word when Victor interrupted. 'Andrew, that's the third time you've woken Lady Matthews. Don't phone again, and by the way, I want to see my newspapers on the street in the morning', and put the phone down on me.

Fortunately for me, it dawned on someone at miners' union HQ that if there weren't newspapers there would be no written coverage of their cause the next morning. Having telephoned their brothers in the print unions to call off the stoppage, I got a phone call to say, 'We're going back to work, Andrew.' Although we lost 250,000 copies that morning we were on the streets in most parts of the country, and Victor was content.

In the midst of the take-over by United Newspapers, Sir Larry had a major heart attack in his office where his life was saved by the quick thinking and action of McGrandle, his deputy, who managed to get him to Bart's within twenty minutes, whereupon he underwent a major emergency by-pass operation. He was out of action for three months and eventually made a complete recovery. But by the time he returned, the new regime was in place. In his opinion he was too professional and proud a man to work with someone like David Stevens, whom he regarded as a City suit with no understanding of newspapers. He left quickly. After the 'Millionaire's Club' circulation uplift, the circulation had started to decline again. I often wonder how different the story of the *Daily Express* would have been if we had had Sir Larry in his prime.

14

THE MILLION-POUND LIBEL CASE

THE *DAILY STAR* was Victor Matthews's baby and he stayed loyal to it through thick and thin and through its various editors. The first editor, Peter Grimsditch, had been replaced by *Express* editor-in-chief Derek Jameson who in due course was followed by Aussie Lloyd Turner, aided and ably abetted by his deputy Brian Hitchen.

In the early days of his editorship, Lloyd Turner benefited from the in-paper Bingo game which the *Daily Star* helped pioneer and which at one stage pushed its share up to 1.7 million. 'We don't need to print newspapers any longer,' Jocelyn once joked to Victor Matthews. 'All we have to do is print Bingo tickets with stories and pictures round them.'

But the *Daily Star*'s rivals, the *Sun* and the *Daily Mirror*, soon caught on and the *Daily Star*'s advantage was lost. Still, Lloyd Turner plugged away producing a paper that, as time went by, lost some of its early cheekiness and sparkle and started to become rather serious and laboured. Doubts were beginning to grow about Turner's editorship when he decided to run a story which was to contribute to him losing his job and the company more than £1 million.

On Sunday 25 October 1986 the *News of the World* ran the head-line 'Tory Boss Archer Pays Vice Girl'. The paper showed a picture of Monica Coghlan, a prostitute who used the name 'Debbie', being 'offered an envelope crammed with £50 notes' by Archer's friend Michael Stacpoole, and it related how the novelist had told Coghlan, 'Go abroad as quickly as you can.'

Over five pages the *NoW* told a complicated tale involving an Asian lawyer named Aziz Kurtha who claimed to have seen Archer going with Coghlan to her hotel near Victoria Station. The *NoW* found Coghlan and over four weeks taped six phone calls she made to Archer. When the story broke, Archer drove from Grantchester to London to see his lawyer Victor, now Lord, Mishcon, who is reported to have asked him three questions. 'Did you sleep with this prostitute?' Archer answered 'No'. 'Have you gone with any other prostitute?' Again the answer was in the negative. 'Do you still want to pursue a political career?' 'Yes', was Archer's reply. 'I have been silly, very foolish,' Archer conceded publicly. 'What else am I to say?' With a general election due just a few months ahead, Mrs Thatcher accepted the resignation of her deputy chairman.

Although anyone reading the *NoW* story would have thought that it implied that Archer had slept with Coghlan, the newspaper was careful not actually to say this. The *Daily Star* of the following Saturday was neither so subtle nor clever. During the previous few days Lloyd Turner had managed to acquire transcripts of the *NoW* phone calls from Coghlan to Archer and also assigned several reporters to try to answer the basic question – why if he had never met her, never mind had sex with her, had he offered her the money?

The 'exclusive' answer provided by the *Daily Star* was headed 'Vice Girl Monica Talks About Archer – The Man She Knew'. Superficially, it looked as though the paper had interviewed Coghlan, although closer inspection indicated that her quotes had been obtained only by speaking to her nephew. The *Star* went much further than the *NoW* in suggesting that the prostitute had slept with Archer and the paper then compounded the damage by saying that 90 per cent of Coghlan's clients 'demand a specialised field of sexual perversion'. 'One of them,' Tony Smith said, 'wanted to be dressed like Little Red Riding Hood, complete with suspenders. He had to be trussed up, and Monica would whip him on the floor of the room.'

Archer moved quickly. He issued libel writs against both the *NoW* and the *Star*, and their respective editors. The two newspapers were heading for a battle with Archer over what the judge would later call 'as big a libel as has ever been tried this century'.

Normally it takes at least two years for a libel action to reach court. This would have meant that the Archer case would not have been heard until the end of 1988. But Archer v Express Newspapers reached the High Court in July 1987, little more than eight months after the *Star* had published its offending article (Archer had argued in a sworn statement that 'I am prevented from any opportunity of resuming my political career'.) In fact, Archer had still kept pretty active politically since issuing his writs, and he tried at first to accelerate the action only against the *Star*, which had gone further than the *NoW* in its allegations. The *Star* was uneasy about how much co-operation it could expect from the *NoW*. In the event both newspapers worked closely together in preparing for the trial.

Archer's QC, Robert Alexander, then 50 years of age, was highly intelligent, had an encyclopaedic memory and considerable charm. He was later to become a peer and chairman of National Westminster Bank. The *Star*'s counsel, Michael Hill, was as distinguished. A former chairman of the Criminal Bar Association, he had a reputation as a tough prosecutor but he had little experience of libel.

Hill certainly put Archer through the hoops. Confronting him with the transcript of his Saturday night conversation with the *News of the World* reporter John Lisners, he put it to Archer that during the conversation Archer 'had lied and lied and lied, did you not?' Archer replied, 'No, sir, and that is grotesquely unfair.'

The *Star's* case was aided by the appearance of Adam Raphael, a distinguished journalist, who was writing for the *Observer* when the story broke. He talked to Archer on the Saturday evening and wrote that Archer had told him that he had met Coghlan 'once only, very casually, about six months ago'. Rupert Morris had claimed the same in *Sunday Today*.

In court, Archer dismissed Raphael's report as 'absolute bunkum' and maintained he had never met Coghlan. But as Raphael pointed out, if Archer had insisted that he had never met Coghlan then he, Raphael, would have put the obvious follow-up question: 'Why on earth, if you've never met this woman, did you pay her off?'

But all this was of little avail in a trial which was stolen by Archer's wife, Mary, who not only looked good but wowed the jury with a superb performance in the witness box, especially when she talked of her 'happy marriage' and confirmed that she and Jeffrey lived what Alexander euphemistically referred to as 'a full life'.

It all went from bad to worse for us. Aziz Kurtha did more harm than good in the witness box while Coghlan's credibility was vulnerable from juvenile convictions for shoplifting and possessing cannabis, quite apart from a long criminal record for prostitution. She had also not been too keen on paying income tax and her social security claims didn't benefit from too close an inspection.

Lloyd Turner was scheduled to appear as the very last witness. But as the trial dragged on, the gloom grew in our camp. Turner knew that if he gave evidence he would have to reveal the source of the *NoW* transcripts which he had obtained in secret and on which his story was based. Turner felt that he owed a duty to Fleet Street to defend himself. But the signs were becoming increasingly ominous and it was obvious that Robert Alexander was going to force him to defend not just the original article but all sorts of totally unrelated items that he might have published, and even material in other tabloids. (These were very much the tactics that John Wilmers QC, acting for the BBC, had adopted in 1984 when he destroyed Derek Jameson, former *Daily Express* editor, who lost his famous libel case against the BBC and its *Week Ending* programme in 1984.)

Two days before he was due in the witness box, Michael Hill and Lord Stevens decided that Turner should not go through with it. They were concerned that he would not be a good performer and could wilt under severe cross-questioning without adding much to the defence. But Turner's silence gave a poor impression and Alexander made the most of it. He mocked 'the silent Mr Lloyd Turner' without mercy. He speculated as to whether Lloyd Turner had 'the power of speech' and wondered whether the *Star* editor suffered from some 'physical infirmity' which prevented him from giving evidence. Legally, there was no reason for Turner to give evidence for he had no direct evidence about whether or not Archer had had sex with Coghlan. But it didn't help our cause.

Nor did Mr Justice Caulfield's summing up. Parts of it have become legal history not because of the perspicacity of his judgment but its histrionic nature. He asked the jury:

'Remember Mary Archer in the witness box. Your vision of her probably will never disappear. Has she elegance? Has she fragrance? Would she have, without the strain of this trial, radiance?' There was a lot more in this vein before he moved on to Archer: 'Is he in need of cold, unloving rubber-insulated sex in a seedy hotel round about quarter to one on a Tuesday morning after an evening at the Caprice?'

Later, much later, when Caulfield died in October 1994, the former Lord Chief Justice Lord Lane, a man who always chose his words with great care even for a lawyer, wrote in an obituary in the *Independent* that Judge Caulfield had the 'occasional irresistible and unresisted impulse to indulge in seemingly pompous hyperbole. This unhappily resulted in judicial pronouncements of questionable fairness and taste …'

The jury returned after four and a quarter hours. They found for Jeffrey Archer and when asked the amount they wished to award for damages (libel juries have that right although settlements today are rather more realistic than they were in the 1980s) the foreman of the jury exclaimed '500,000 pounds'.

The £500,000 was a new British record. On top of that we had to pay around £700,000 to cover both sides' costs. Stevens put a brave face on it. 'It's been quite an expensive day, hasn't it?' he said as he poured drinks to the team returning from court. There was also a 'defeat dinner' to keep the spirits up – and flowing. At first, we wanted to appeal. Michael Hill felt, in particular, that Judge Caulfield's summing up gave us good grounds for a retrial. But gradually reality seeped in. It would be almost impossible to get Coghlan back into the witness box and, even so, she had been pretty disastrous to our cause. We feared that a retrial might double our legal bill without any real guarantee that the outcome would be any better. Reluctantly, we dropped the idea of an appeal. Shortly afterwards the *News of the World* settled their dispute out of court, paying Archer £50,000 damages and £30,000 costs.

A few weeks after the Archer trial, Lloyd Turner resigned as editor of the *Daily Star* and ushered in the short-lived and disastrous regime of Mike 'Bonking' Gabbert.

15

THE 'FREELLOYDERS'

IN THE SHORT PERIOD of Roger Boase's tenancy as managing director of Express Newspapers he was charged by David Stevens with finding a new editor for the *Daily Express*. There was an interregnum, capably handled by Leith McGrandle, the deputy editor. Boase had heard rumours that Nicholas Lloyd, then part of the News International team who had been editor of the *News of the World* during its transition from broadsheet to tabloid format, was being groomed for 'greater things'.

Lloyd was courted by Boase at the opera, and was duly hired. Nicholas Lloyd was in many ways a typical 'creative' type, a nice man, but somewhat insecure. Of medium height, with an almost impish face, he was clever and urbane. A great man for networking, his dinner parties were legendary, attended by many of the great and good from the world of politics and show business. He was a delightful host and his wife Eve Pollard, who could be formidable professionally, would be absolutely charming on such occasions and great fun.

Politically, Nicholas was a hard-line Tory, a Thatcherite when she was in power, who became a confirmed Majorite when his erstwhile heroine was ousted and John Major moved into Number 10. In fact, it was his dedication to the interests of the Tory party which was eventually to play a significant contribution in his downfall. Regardless of merit, Lloyd's pursuit of Tory party interests – through the columns of the *Daily Express* – was paramount. Indeed, at one party conference he was overheard saying to a cabinet minister, 'How are we doing?' Not 'How are you doing?'

This emphasis on 'we' was disturbing when all the research carried out on *Daily Express* readers showed that they expected the newspaper to be Tory, but with a small 't'. They wanted sensible, constructive criticism of the government of the day, and a sharp wrist-slapping where it was due. As a traditionally conservative but not Conservative paper, the *Express* has historically been able to fulfil this role. Tory governments tend to listen more keenly to criticism from those they know to be their friends, albeit not uncritical ones. *Daily Express* headlines about just how well the country was doing during the late 1980s and early 1990s did not go down well with the paper's bedrock readers, including the self-employed small businessman and the hard-pressed middle-class men and women readers who were becoming increasingly disillusioned with the Tory government. During the Lloyd period I believe that the *Daily Express* lost credibility amongst thousands of readers. You treat your readers as fools at your peril, and sadly, that is what we seemed to be doing.

Nicholas could be petulant, almost a member of the quivering lip brigade, when you had a row. I remember during one such altercation he said to me, 'I would remind you that I was knighted by Margaret Thatcher for my services to journalism.' Delusions of grandeur on these lines were worrying. Mrs Thatcher had, in essence, 'knighted' the editor of the *Daily Express* for the newspaper's devotion to the Tory cause during her premiership.

If only Mrs Thatcher had known what was afoot at the *Daily Express* during the last days before her disembowelment by her parliamentary colleagues in late 1991. David Stevens and I discovered that the *Daily Express* was about to run a front page with the headline – 'It must be Heseltine'. David Stevens had to instruct Lloyd to continue supporting Mrs Thatcher as Prime Minister and Conservative Party leader. Rightly he claimed that it would be crazy to change horses in midstream – our readers would have wondered what on earth was going on for the majority of middle-class, middle England remained fairly staunch supporters of the Iron Lady.

At the 1993 general election Nicholas's views on the outcome caused fluttering in the Lloyds' North London dovecote. He felt that Labour, then led by Neil Kinnock, could squeak into power by a narrow majority, and he was very concerned about the effect this might have on the fortunes of the highly paid (but not all the highly paid, just the editors of the *Express* titles). He wrote a letter to me expressing the biggest worry on his mind. Would it be possible, he wondered, to trade in his Jaguar for a smaller car and convert the balance to salary? Was there any way, he asked, if a goodly portion of his salary could be paid offshore through one of United Newspapers' many overseas subsidiaries? This was a stunning suggestion by the editor of a newspaper who would be among the first to attack any such proposals among the wealthier of the masses. I mentioned Lloyd's proposal to David Stevens, who was not amused either by the approach or the faint-hearted attitude in the face of the socialist enemy on the election battlefield.

Probably the biggest mistake David Stevens and I made in our quest for editorial nirvana was to hire the other half of the Lloyd duo – Eve Pollard, later to become 'Lady Lloyd' – as editor of the *Sunday Express*. She was especially admired by the United hierarchy as editor of the *Sunday Mirror*, and I was instructed to pursue her relentlessly, which I did. I was pushing on a fairly open door because her husband had for some time been canvassing the hierarchy with the idea of a 'dream ticket' of the two Lloyds at the two *Expresses*.

I like Eve very much socially, but as an editor, although she bounced with creative ideas, she was, like many editors, a poor judge of people, and an appalling manager of staff. In fact the appointment of Caligula would, according to many male staff, have been preferable. She was the world's greatest emasculator, who could, and did, reduce strong men to tears – no easy task in the hard-faced world of national newspaper journalism. Living in her rarefied world, she forgot, or had never learned, that when grown men quivered in her presence and put up with her tongue-lashings and tantrums, they were prevented by their domestic circumstances from doing what they really wanted to do and telling her to 'stick it'. They had wives and families or other dependants. Their circumstances in no way could be compared with the grand lifestyle of Fleet Street's 'dynamic duo'. Family circumstances made them vulnerable. She just thought that they were weak.

She also carried out some bizarre activities. She had seen a pair of shoes she fancied in Oxford Street, but couldn't remember where. A photographer was dispatched on a Saturday morning to take pictures of each shoe-shop window until the objects of her desire were identified. It wasn't only the men who suffered. Eve got through 30-plus secretaries during her three years of editorship. She treated them appallingly, hurling clothes on to the floor when she changed to go out, ordering them to 'pick them up'. If she fancied a drink of mineral water she would yell, 'Fizz, girl!'

As a duo the Lloyds were pretty deadly as employees, despite giving myself and David Stevens absolute undertakings that they would never work in 'concert'. There was the alleged scandal of the refurbishment and decoration of the Pollard villa in the south of France, as reported in *Private Eye*, which coincided with a fine article on refurbishing villas in that region of France in the *Sunday Express Classic* magazine.

One of the staff told me that *Sunday Express* journalistic rumour had it that, when questions began to be asked, Eve's loyal chauffeur was seen to be carrying away some samples of paint. Unfortunately the poor man dropped one outside the lawyer's office and it burst all over the floor. Panic ensued, and a major clear-up operation frantically took place. The balance of the unspilled material was rumoured to have found its way on to a West London rubbish dump.

Free holidays provided by companies seeking editorial publicity for their glamorous destinations were much sought after, first class of course, with the West Indies a firm favourite. 'Freebies', as they are known in the newspaper business, are normally extended by travel companies to travel writers who are given free journeys and hospitality in exchange for an 'independent' travel piece extolling the virtues of the host company's destination. They have been around for a long time although during the Beaverbrook regime, and for some time after he died, freebies were banned by Express Newspapers much to the chagrin of *Express* journalists.

On one occasion, an *Express* financial journalist had, without permission, gone off on a freebie to Bermuda where a City travel company was opening a new hotel. The reception was magnificent, the food succulent and the booze flowed freely. The weary but hard-working hacks finally made it back to their hotel bedrooms just before the Caribbean dawn. Suddenly, pandemonium broke out. News had reached the hotel that the governor of Bermuda, Sir Richard Sharples, a former Tory minister, had been assassinated in the grounds of Government House. Within minutes, the 'tired and emotional' cream of Fleet Street had descended on the one-man police station demanding to have 'all the facts'. It was a big enough nightmare for the unfortunate policeman to have a murdered governor on his hands; to have the hounds of Fleet Street snapping at his heels was more than anyone deserved.

The intrepid *Express* newshound was in a dilemma. If he filed an 'our man on the spot' news piece it would reveal that he was enjoying a forbidden freebie. If he failed to file, he would be passing up one of the biggest news stories of the month, if not the year. Sensibly, perhaps, he put his journalistic news sense to one side, hired a boat and spent the day fishing while his colleagues kept the wires burning between Bermuda and Fleet Street.

But by the time the Lloyds, or the 'FreeLloyders', as *Private Eye* called them, were *in situ* at the Black Lubyanka, the anti-freebie days at the *Express* had long since gone. The whole freebie racket had got out of hand with the travel writers being leant on by the hierarchy to obtain goodies for their bosses – the feature editors and, ultimately, the editor – and sometimes their spouses. There was one famous occasion where a fashion shoot in the West Indies took place while the Lloyds were in attendance on holiday. This was, I believe, the occasion when Andrew Neil was snapped in the arms of the dusky beauty so familiar to *Private Eye* readers.

The Lloyds worked remorselessly to extract more and more publicity expenditure from the *Express* board to promote their titles. They claimed that the sickly, sinking sales figures could be put right at a stroke by pouring money into television advertising. It never seemed to occur that there might be something amiss with the editorial content of the titles.

Although, despite this, I had some sympathy with their desire for more money for promotional activity, I had to be realistic in the interests of United Newspapers. Besides, David Stevens didn't like television advertising anyway as he felt it was a great waste of money, an attitude which led to a number of arguments not only with the Lloyds but other editors.

Not that Express Newspapers' promotional budget was minuscule. At the time the Lloyds were clamouring for more and more money for this purpose, the group's promotional budget was already over £20 million per annum. Express Newspapers' titles were always heavily outgunned by a far wealthier opposition and much fierce debate took place at Express board meetings on this subject.

But one method employed by Eve Pollard to promote the *Sunday Express* cause was totally unacceptable and could, perhaps should, have led to her dismissal for gross misconduct. Pollard instructed Charles Golding, her odious deputy editor at the *Sunday Express*, to try to set up the board of the company at the interim results meeting by getting awkward questions asked by analysts. It all started in the City office of the *Sunday Express*, then run by one Dominic Prince, a notorious City journalist of fearsome reputation. A casual journalist, an attractive young female, received a telephone call from the devious Golding, instructing her to phone investment managers she knew in the City and ask them to pose awkward questions about the company's invest-ment policy towards the *Sunday Express* at the United Newspapers' interim results meeting, in a deliberate attempt to embarrass the chairman, Lord Stevens.

The young journalist was so frightened that she informed Prince, who came to see me, sweating copiously at the act of shopping his boss. I took him to see Lord Stevens and I gave my word to Prince that the girl would be looked after, and repeated the promise when she came to see me shortly afterwards. She was genuinely terrified of Golding and of what might happen to her, and I moved her to the *Daily Star*, with the then editor Brian Hitchen's approval, to keep her out of harm's way. She repeated exactly what she had been asked to do by Golding and wrote down and signed a statement.

I got into my car and went to Golding's house in Hampstead accompanied by the personnel director, Struan Coupar. Golding's wife came to the door and said that he was unwell with a migraine. I insisted on seeing him and was shown into the sitting room. Golding appeared in his dressing-gown and, admittedly, looked distinctly off colour. I tape-recorded the conversation. When, following intense interrogation, he finally admitted his part in the plot, Golding made the rather strange statement, 'I plead the Eichmann defence' – an odd remark for a man who wore his Jewish faith so proudly. But we knew what he meant: I was only obeying orders. Golding was fired, but not before trying to blacken the young journalist's character about her private life with lies about her trying to seduce him. In fact, she told me that it was he who had made the attempt by pouncing on her in the lift one day and forcing his tongue into her mouth.

Pollard got away with it even though she was 'banged to rights', in common parlance, but she had lost her mentor and hatchet man. Golding had ruled as her deputy by fear. His office overlooked Blackfriars Bridge and he would sit with binoculars watching staff come back from lunch, and report those he felt to be late to Eve, who would instruct him to take appropriate action which he would relish. When staff were being interviewed about the 'interim results' affair, they were guaranteed by me that there would be no retribution. They could talk freely. Golding knew the position and threatened them anyway, and they were extremely reluctant to talk. Golding had to be 'spoken to' and desisted rapidly until the conclusion of the investigation.

I went to David Stevens to discuss whether to dismiss Pollard. Geoffrey Ampthill, deputy chairman, always impressed by an ample bosom, left the bar at the House of Lords to speak eloquently in defence of Pollard arguing that, above all, we should avoid a scandal, which he felt would 'harm the company and David Stevens's reputation'. After all, the wily Ampthill went on, hadn't there been enough damage done to the company, albeit unwarranted, over the Maxwell affair, David Sullivan et al? Pollard stayed and went on with Nicholas Lloyd, it was heavily rumoured in the City, to attempt to put together a 'buy out' of the Express Group, accompanied by one of the Saatchi brothers. The Lloyd 'buy out' plan was never taken seriously by the City.

Both Lloyds lost their editorships in fairly quick succession. Pollard went on to co-write a successful novel and Sir Nicholas began a new career in public relations.

16

BRIAN HITCHEN
British Bulldog

BRIAN HITCHEN, who succeeded Eve Pollard as editor of the *Sunday Express*, took pride in regarding himself as being to the right of Ghengis Khan. And he wasn't far wrong. The scourge of yobs and scroungers, a dedicated Tory supporter, a supporter of capital punishment – he was 'hang and flog 'em Brian'.

Short, bald, with a broad shiny face and a winning smile, Brian was a great news-hound and a reporter of the old school. He had been around Fleet Street for many years, including a stint as editor of the *Daily Star*, from which he was plucked to become the fourth editor of the *Sunday Express* since Junor left in 1989.

I first met Brian when he was news editor of the *Daily Express* in the mid-1970s under editor Iain McColl, when he was heavily involved in the pursuit of Great Train Robber, Ronnie Biggs. When the TV film of this event was made, Brian's role featured strongly as a hard-edged newsman.

When he had worked for the *Daily Mirror* some years earlier as a foreign correspondent, he covered many of the world's hot spots, including the Vietnam War, and saw much suffering and misery. He had himself suffered some pain and misery when, in only his early forties, he was waiting at an airport to go on yet another foreign assignment when he felt very unwell. He got into his car and drove to his doctor, who listened to his chest, and told him not to move. He was whisked into hospital to have an immediate quadruple heart bypass.

Twenty years later, he is still going strong, smoking enormous cigars with relish and downing whiskies of a true Irish measure. His attitude to life is that after what he's seen and done, you've got to go sometime – and of something; he and the late Robert Mitchum could have been soul mates.

He was a fine friend, loyal and honourable, and I loved him dearly. He could be reduced to tears by an emotional story about bravery. He supported his staff through thick and thin, pleading for their jobs even when someone was caught fiddling. On one occasion a photographer was dismissed never to darken our doors again. I found out that Brian continued to commission him and he was paid in cash in a brown envelope. He found it difficult to see bad in any journalist.

His views on managers and proprietors were somewhat different. He viewed them with distaste and suspicion, believing that little but incompetence and stupidity prevailed. He particularly disliked Lord Ampthill, the deputy chairman of United Newspapers, whom he believed was the source of his undoing as editor of the *Sunday Express*. Ampthill was the centre of the controversial 'baby in the bath' case in which it was argued that although his parents had never consummated their marriage, his mother had conceived him by the sperm left in his father's bath water. The court found in his favour and he gained the peerage. He felt that Ampthill was not only devious in his own interests but also Machiavellian. There always appeared to be an ulterior motive in everything Ampthill did.

Indeed, Ampthill was also instrumental in my undoing, telling Hollick that I was no doubt a competent general manager but would never be a good managing director. This from a man who never held down a proper job for more than five minutes in his entire life. Ampthill, and people like him from the hereditary peerage stable, have to be one of the best reasons for getting rid of the House of Lords.

Brian was a great supporter of the military and virtually adopted the Parachute Regiment whose exploits he greatly admired, even having a large painting in his office of the paras in action. A large Union Jack held pride of place next to his desk. His straight-speaking attitude never came to light more strongly than when, after he became editor of the *Daily Star*, a meeting was held with our partners from Ireland, with whom we jointly produced a version of the *Daily Star* based much on sport and with no tits, as befits a good Catholic country.

After the association with Gabbert, the paper was failing miserably, and I was summoned to a meeting with Jerry McGuinness and John Meagher of our partners in Ireland at an out-of-the-way restaurant in Dun Laoghaire outside Dublin to decide what to do. We decided not to close the Irish title but to persist and endeavour to improve its editorial quality and coverage.

At the next board meeting held in London, which included the Irish editor and directors, Brian launched a vitriolic attack on them, the substance of which was that editorially the newspaper was a 'crock of shit'.

'Why don't you say what you really mean, Brian?' said someone in an endeavour to defuse the tension which was building rapidly into a possible declaration of hostilities by both sides. Things calmed down, and a new policy was agreed, with Brian having the final say.

Brian did a fine job on the *Star*, turning it rapidly back into a 'proper' newspaper, but much damage was done, and it took a huge amount of work. Brian always expressed pride in his paper, regardless of how he really felt – a real professional.

A most complex situation arose with Mohamed Al Fayed, of Harrods fame, in his never ending pursuit of the elusive British citizenship he still seeks with desperation, pursuing every possible avenue of attack.

Fayed's devotion to children, and especially handicapped children, is well known and genuine. Each Christmas the *Daily Star* would hold a party in the office for children from the Royal Marsden Hospital. Fayed would invariably turn up not only with presents for the children, but would play with them for hours – this was a really genuine side of the man. There was no publicity involved around these activities.

Brian, in fact, originally met Fayed when raising money for the children's unit of the Royal Marsden. Almost immediately, Fayed wrote out a cheque for £265,000 to buy an operating theatre for the department. He also gave Brian an open-ended guarantee that there was more money available, as long as Brian did not reveal where the money came from. Brian and I felt that Fayed was a true friend of the *Daily Star* and admired him for that.

It was not unusual for the flamboyant owner of Harrods to call Brian's residence or office at all sorts of odd times. One Sunday morning Fayed telephoned Brian at his Sussex home. 'Listen very carefully, my friend,' said Fayed as he came on the line. 'I have something for you that is very big ... I want to tell you about those thieving bastard politicians who are surrounding John Major and I want to tell you about the corruption that is going on and that nobody knows about.'

He went on: 'I'll tell you about a cabinet minister who took a one-million-pound bribe from Tiny Rowland and about another who runs escort agencies for Arabs; and about how the Thatcher family has salted away money in numbered Swiss bank accounts ... And I'll tell you about crooked lobbyists who hawk bent MPs around who will ask questions in Parliament if you give them enough money to be on your side, and then tell you to fuck off when they are climbing the career ladder and don't want to know a poor old wog anymore ... I'm going to blow the whole lot of them out of the water. You are editor of the *Sunday Express*. You can show these people for what they are. Bloody parasites.

'I don't want to hurt John Major. He's a decent man. Least I think so. But he's got to be told about the bastards surrounding him. Crooked swine. I have all the evidence you need. Meet me on Tuesday at 5 o'clock. It will blow your mind, my friend. I not tell anyone else. We have a deal. You get big exclusive. See you then.'

At the appointed hour on Tuesday 24 September, Brian arrived at Fayed's private offices at Harrods. 'Sit down, sit down ... how you bin? I tell you before of those swindling bastard MPs and those crooks in parliament. They take my money and spit in my face. Eh, they think they are dealing with a wog. That's how they think of me. A rich wog. Well, have I got news for those bastards ... Let's start with Neil Hamilton. That bastard has had thousands out of me. I help him out because he needs money. He help me out because he ask questions in the House for me about the takeover of Harrods. Ian Greer, the lobby guy, he fix Hamilton up for me. If I pay him. I had to have somebody ask questions for me. Every other bastard is on the side of Tiny Rowland. And then when I wrote a letter of congratulations to Neil Hamilton when he was made a minister he told me never to contact him at the office again. He took my money and now doesn't want to know me. How's that for gratitude? It was all right when he needed me. Now he wants to keep his distance from me. What they think I have, the plague?

'The government and civil servants, they block my application for citizenship, even though my children were born here. I employ 10,000 people, I pay £8 million personal income tax and £30 million corporation tax. I pay my way in this country. What are they trying to do to me? The French, they are begging me to be a French citizen. I own the Duke of Windsor's house in Paris. They have even offered to make me a count. But I don't want to be French. I want to be British. Why can't anyone understand that? I know you understand, because you are proud of being British. Like I would be.

'I'll tell you about Tiny Rowland and where I got the evidence that is going to blow some people out of the water. After we made the peace in the food hall with that shark I'd labelled "Tiny", we came up here and sat in this room and I asked him to tell me the truth about how he had double-crossed me and what dirty tricks he had pulled against me to get me discredited and for that lousy Department of Trade and Industry Report to be made against me.

'Rowland told me everything. He told me how he had paid two ex-Scotland yard men £1 million between them to bend that report. He tell me all these things himself, sitting right here in this office. I put a tape recorder on the table and asked Tiny to tell me about it. What it matter anymore? It not matter anymore. That's what I thought anyway. He told me he had given a man £1 million to pass on to a cabinet minister to stop me getting British citizenship, and he did. That's why I still can't get British citizenship, even though I feel more English than most of the people who were born here. I love this country. The biggest British flag flies every day over Harrods. Yet politicians take my money and spit in my face.

'Jonathan Aitken ... he's a minister and he's supposed to be selling armaments to the Arabs. Yet he's staying at the Ritz in Paris and the Saudis are picking up the bill. How do I know? Because I own the Ritz. You know that. That's how I know these things. He procures women for Arabs. He has interests in a model agency in Paris. He provides hookers for Arabs and gets to sell arms to Arabs. I'll give you a stack of names of MPs who have stayed at the Ritz for free. Then, suddenly they don't want to know me. They charge everything to their rooms. Cashmere sweaters, ties, all sorts of things. I've had MPs coming here and saying, "I'm going on a fact-finding mission to somewhere and thought it would be flying the flag if I wore a Harrods suit." "You want a suit?" I say, "I give you a suit." Then they want shirts and ties. Cheapskate bastards are just freeloaders.'

Brian came back to the office and told both Lord Stevens and myself of Fayed's intention to release the information on alleged corruption among senior members of the government. (This was the first hint of the sleaze scandal to come and which was to plague the already weak Major government until its overwhelming defeat in the general election of 1 May 1997.) Lord Stevens didn't want to rush at it, but both Brian and I felt that the Prime Minister should know about the impending scandal. So Brian telephoned Downing Street and was granted an interview that very evening.

He met the Prime Minister and his press secretary in private. Both listened and thanked him for coming to see them. Then the duplicity started. 'Leaks' about 'go betweens' intervening on behalf of Fayed were published, with speculation that Hitchen was the man. Brian was never a 'go between'. He believed he was doing the right thing to protect the Prime Minister.

The next day Brian came to see me. A package had arrived from Harrods – a fob watch as a gift of friendship from Fayed. (I'd have been a bit pissed off it wasn't a Rolex, even though it would have gone back immediately). I wrote a note to Brian and kept a copy in my safe describing exactly what had happened, and Brian passed the watch into my care.

When Pollard left the company, Brian was, in my view, the only choice for editor. The morale of the *Sunday Express* staff was at an all-time low. They had been pounded and emasculated, denigrated and crucified. They needed a strong leader to restore their confidence, and Brian set about this task with gusto. Very soon morale was high and the paper moving in a positive direction. We just had to keep his love of all things military under control!

In 1995 it was decided that the *Daily Express* needed a change of editor. When circulation figures don't go well, regardless of the reasons, the fall guy is always the editor. Applications were sought, and secret meetings took place with those who had applied.

Two seemed outstanding: Richard Addis and Susan Douglas. It was at this point that Ampthill, the deputy chairman, who had long had the knife out for Brian, decided, as Brian was within a year of retirement, that we should revitalise both the *Daily* and *Sunday Express* at the same time by appointing two young editors.

I insisted on telling Brian of the decision myself. His reaction was predictable and gentlemanly, though the words about the choice of his successor are unprintable. In fact Susan Douglas did not last long as *Sunday Express* editor, and Richard Addis, *Daily Express* editor for only a year more, ended up editing both newspapers – the *Daily Express*, cunningly renamed the *Express*, and the *Sunday Express*, apeing its more successful Associated rival, now titled the *Express on Sunday*

17

THE LOST TRIBES
OF FLEET STREET

I WAS AT A PARTY once in the mid-80s when trade union domination in Fleet Street was at its most powerful. Someone heard that I was a newspaper manager and asked me:

'Is it as bad as people say? What are the unions really like?'

The answer to the first question was easy – 'No, it's worse.'

To answer the second question I used a comparison with African tribal society which had often occurred to me in the long, weary hours I and many others used to spend 'negotiating' with the various warring factions of the print unions. African countries are usually split into regions in which major dominant tribes of ancient lineage mingle with a multiplicity of other tribes who form alliances, break alliances and fall out with one another and themselves. As in Nigeria, for example, with the mighty Hausa, the Yoruba and the Ibo tribes, although even within these great tribes there are sub-tribes and a myriad of smaller unrelated tribes who form shifting alliances with them.

Territory is vital to the structure of African tribal society. So is tradition. And there is a strict hierarchy with one tribe looking down on the tribe below it, who in turn look down on an inferior tribe. (Rather like the classic 'upper, middle and working class' comic sketch by Cleese/Barker/Corbett.)

So it was with the tribes of Fleet Street.

Everyone working in the print trade had to be unionised. The union card was the passport to the riches of Fleet Street. To lose your union card was to lose your livelihood. Without it, finding another job in the print trade would be impossible and even getting a job outside the trade would be very difficult. Print union membership ran in families – just as it did in all the great traditional industries such as mining and the docks. Son would follow father into the trade and daughters would often be found a job, usually as a secretary, in a newspaper.

The traditions of the leading print unions are rooted in history. Many of the men and women who worked in the print trade were sincere and hard-working. But as the power of the union leadership grew, the general rank-and-file became increasingly powerless to do much else but follow union orders.

Since, within the umbrella of a single union, there would be individual chapels for every section of the trade, the numbers of workers involved were often small. Loyalty was primarily to your local chapel, then to the members of your union in the same newspaper, then to your fellow union members in different newspapers.

Turf wars within the same union and between unions in the same newspaper were fought on a constant basis. New machinery provided fertile ground for breeding 'who does what' disputes. For example, the smallest problem with an ink pump, situated at the top of the press, would involve six men. There would be an engineer and his assistant to cope with the hydraulics, an electrician and his assistant to deal with the electrical switches, and a plumber and his assistant to handle any problem with the piping (his assistant would also hold the ladder when required).

A concession granted to one chapel (union section) would be instantly demanded by chapels in the same union on the same newspaper. Anything granted then to one union would form the basis of a claim by rival unions.

The power of the 'father of the chapel' or 'mother of the chapel' who held the union cards of their members was considerable. Although most of the chapel officials were men there were a number of formidable 'mothers' whose ferocity and Marxist orthodoxy would shame most of their male counterparts. The power of a 'father' or 'mother' depended on the numbers and negotiation power of their chapel (i.e. how easy it was for their chapel to bring the newspaper to a halt by withdrawing their 'co-operation'). However, even the most powerful 'father' of a less superior union such as NATSOPA were of lower 'status' than a middle-ranking official in a superior print union like the NGA. The NGA composing chapels had their own 'imperial father'. And, towering over the whole structure was the 'federated house father' who always came from the ranks of the NGA, the aristocrats of the printing trade, and who was effectively the paramount chief. Yet even he was still unable to control individual 'fathers' because the constituent parts of the federated house chapel were drawn from all the different chapels, skilled and unskilled – they could hardly sit at the same table together, let alone agree a policy.

When an inter-chapel war broke out or bad blood emerged between two different unions within the same newspaper, the dispute would be passed up to the officials of the local branch. And if the branch could not settle the matter then the national officers would be called in.

The rank-and-file union members, most of whom took a pride in their work and just wanted to get on with their job, were too often caught in this tangled web – as was the newspaper manager. As the union power craze reached its height, it was the ordinary rank-and-file members who increasingly became the victims of their union leadership. In the end most of them paid with their jobs and livelihood. There was no place for them when the Fleet Street revolution took place.

Here is a brief layman's guide to the formerly great print union tribes which once wielded such power and now are either extinct, have merged or are only a shadow of their former selves. These were the main unions as they were known in the 1970s and 1980s. Some unions, such as the Monotype Casters' and Typefounders' Society, the London Typographical Society and the Association of Correctors of the Press, had already been swallowed up.

AUEW Engineers – Amalgamated Union of Engineering Workers
This union grew more powerful with the increased mechanisation of Fleet Street. The duties involved all engineering work including equipment breakdown, preventative maintenance, workshop engineering, installation work, plumbing (plus apprentices).

EETPU Electricians – Electrical and Electronic Technicians'
and Plumbers' Union As with the engineers, mechanisation brought more power to the leaders of the electricians' union. Their members' duties included all electric and electronic repair work, maintenance and installation work, but their responsibilities did not cover plumbing in newspaper plants which lay in the powers of the AUEW.

EETPU Assistants – as above The duties involved the unskilled assistants to the above, plus apprentices. The assistants tended to carry the electrician's tool bag and, in theory, hand him the screwdriver.

IOJ – Institute of Journalists A weaker alternative to the National Union of Journalists (NUJ). Rather genteel, non-militant, manned by the pipe-smoking, corduroy-wearing tendency.

NGA – National Graphical Association The NGA were known as the 'gentlemen of the press'. They could, and often did, trace their roots back to the medieval guilds. The NGA was the craft union and an apprenticeship in the trade was a requirement. There were many different areas of the newspaper industry covered by the NGA but the main duties included all typesetting; Linotype operators, time or stone hands, case ship operators, readers, printing machine-minders, foundry workers, telecommunications workers, skilled publishing room workers.

NATSOPA – National Association of Printers' Assistants Assistants to the NGA craft union. In the main their ranks included composing room proof pullers, readers' assistants, telephone reporters, messengers, clerical staff, secretaries, engineers' assistants, printing machine assistants, photographic dark room operatives, librarians, cleaners, canteen staff, clerical assistants, publishing room assistants.

NUJ – National Union of Journalists Writers, reporters, photographers, sub-editors, specialist writers – militant union, loathed by most working journalists and manned at branch and national levels on the whole by journalists who couldn't hack it anywhere else.

SLADE – Society of Lithographic Artists, Designers, Engravers and Process Workers The SLADE duties included etching process plates for picture reproduction, studio artwork for publicity, advertising, and outdoor and indoor events.

SOGAT – Society of Graphic and Allied Trades Like NATSOPA, a bit of a 'catch-all' union whose members included warehouse men, drivers, circulation reps, chauffeurs, van loaders and distributors.

18

THE TYRANNY OF 'THE BROTHERS'

'THERE ARE THE TRADE UNIONISTS, once the oppressed now the tyrants, whose selfish and sectional pretensions need to be bravely opposed.'

The distinguished economist Maynard Keynes wrote these prescient words in 1926, when Britain was brought to a standstill by the might of the trade unions united in the General Strike. Fifty odd years later in Fleet Street, Keynes's warning was to haunt the managements of Britain's national newspapers as they grappled with the trade union tyrants in a morass largely of their own making. For although Fleet Street managements recognised that the despotism of the print unions had to be 'bravely opposed', the will to challenge the people who could instantly stop their newspapers – and their cash flows – was conspicuously absent.

The print unions generally stood united in their ever increasing, ever more exorbitant demands, while the managements were so divided by the ever-present threat of non-production that they fell, paralysed by fear, into a web of deceit and dishonesty that inevitably lay behind so many of the regular 'quick fix' settlements.

Brave hearts like Victor Matthews tried to introduce a measure of sanity into the Fleet Street mess and he made some progress. But he was a man ahead of his time and there was a limit to the impact that even a man as determined as Matthews could do to ease the stranglehold of the unions. Matthews made a start – but that is all.

The avarice of the print unions knew few bounds. But their greed was matched and nurtured by management weakness, incompetence and profligacy on a scale which beggars belief now, even as it did, for those in the know, at the time.

This combination of forces had, by the early 1980s, put the print workers at the summit of earnings within the trade union movement. Their pay rates were the source of envy of other trade unionists and the subject of utter amazement to any outside observers who came anywhere near to knowing the truth about the Fleet Street jungle.

By the mid-1980s, newspaper managements were completely at the mercy of the print unions. The 'threat to strike' gun was kept permanently cocked. All too often the gun was fired, on the flimsiest of excuses, and newspapers, or at least certain editions, failed to appear. The price of reappearance was invariably high, starting with the reinstatement of the offending chapel. In addition its members – plus anyone else affected – would demand, and be paid, 'catch-up' money to do the work they should have done in the first place before they went on strike. These weak and flaccid settlements almost inevitably led to yet another claim by yet another union, or even sections of the same union. The result was business anarchy and economic insanity.

The nature of newspapers – with a shelf life of hours – meant that an edition lost could never be retrieved. The perishability of the products of the newspaper industry made newspaper managements, at the height of the trade union tyranny, especially vulnerable to threats which would too readily lead to appeasement and surrender.

Yet, although the abuses of the 'blue collar' print workers are now notorious and legendary, in my experience we had more industrial trouble from the 'white collar' self-styled 'gentlemen of the press', the National Union of Journalists (NUJ).

The closure of the *Scottish Daily Express* plant in Glasgow, for example, was largely a result of the NUJ's doing, even if the root cause of their members' discontent lay in the hugely inflated wage levels of the print workers. Some of these men in the London composing room piece-work sections were taking home more than £50,000 a year for an official 26-hour week (it was often much less). This was at least double the pay of the average sub-editor for working two-thirds of a sub's working hours.

In Glasgow there were 56 stoppages in production in 52 weeks, and despite a desperate plea for peace from the then managing director, Jocelyn Stevens, he was met by the intransigent words from the NUJ: 'If you want to print newspapers in Scotland, you pay our fucking price.'

The price was too high. But the *Daily Express* is still paying for it – even though the Glasgow plant was closed and 1800 jobs lost. Printing of the *Scottish Daily Express* was moved to Manchester, but the real cost was incalculable for patriotic Scottish readers deserted the 'English' newspaper in their hundreds of thousands.

Eventually in 1996, the *Scottish Daily Express* returned to Scotland, printed under contract by D. C. Thomson in Glasgow. The paper itself was also produced in Glasgow instead of being transmitted from London or Manchester. But the damage had been done and a newspaper which had proudly sold over 650,000 copies a day (in a population of five million, second only to the *Daily Record*), is now struggling along with a circulation of around 100,000 and facing fierce competition from other English titles, notably *The Sun* and *Daily Mail* which rushed to fill the vacuum and now print in Glasgow.

By the mid-1980s the situation had reached almost complete anarchy and the managements of Britain's national newspapers were managers in name only. The power of the unions was virtually total and their refusal to embrace any kind of new technology without demanding extortionate settlements was unflinching. As a result, newspaper type was still being set in hot metal on Linotype machines which had been invented almost a century earlier. The mighty printing presses which shook the whole building as they thundered into action at night (unions allowing) were almost as old. At their best they could churn out hundreds of thousands of copies a night, albeit at the reduced output on which the machine unions insisted. Most of the presses were designed and capable of producing 60,000 copies an hour but were limited to whatever was currently the agreed figure with the union – usually less than half their capacity.

Letterpress machines lacked the ability to produce colour, other than 'spot' colour in red or on predetermined spaces such as the front and back pages. Occasionally, special events demanded special measures and on these occasions special photogravure colour pages were printed at other printing plants and fed into the presses on the night of production. It was an operation fraught with peril and frequently led to lost editions as every union chapel directly or even remotely connected with the printing operation dipped their bread into the 'colour' gravy.

Despite the pressures that newspaper managements were under, they did not lack imagination. On one occasion, in the early days of absorbent blue J-cloths, someone had the bright idea of running whole reels of J-cloths in conjunction with the newsprint to produce a *Daily Express* J-cloth special. Whether due to technical problems, or union sabotage, the whole operation was a disaster. Very few readers received their copy of the *Daily Express* with free J-cloth enclosed. But it was general knowledge that many families in the East End of London had no need to buy J-cloths for a decade or more afterwards.

At Express Newspapers alone, there were 43 negotiating sections in London, 42 in Manchester and nine remaining in the ashes of Glasgow. Each of these print and clerical sections were tied to the others by differential pay structures of labyrinthine complexity, the legacies of countless settlements over the decades. Any single one of them could hold the company to ransom by the threat of non-production and the unions' 'power of veto' was invoked constantly.

Opposing them, more in theory than in practice, was the Newspapers Publishers' Association (NPA), which represented the Fleet Street owners and their managements and which spent most of its time on industrial relations problems. But the NPA was fatally flawed, for the only real weapon it could wield was union-style solidarity among publishers. If one newspaper was suffering from a strike then, the theory ran, all members of the NPA should give support to the victim.

The result was quite the opposite. There was no 'Three Musketeers' spirit in Fleet Street management, no 'all for one and one for all'. It was more a case of 'every man for himself and the devil take the hindmost'. Once word went round Fleet Street that a newspaper faced industrial action and its production was threatened, the others would invariably gather to feast on the stricken beast. Print times would be brought forward and editions scrapped; print orders would be increased by hundreds of thousands of copies and papers would be produced throughout the night (at the cost of additional payments to the unions). The unions knew this management weakness was one of their greatest weapons, and took maximum advantage of their employers' stupidity.

Union chapels had since the 1960s won the right to drive their own deals with their own newspaper proprietors. The NPA rarely figured in negotiations on wages or conditions nor did the national union bosses (although the latter sometimes intervened in industrial disputes, occasionally on the side of common sense if they felt a local chapel had got wildly out of line).

The annual NPA wage deal provided the theory but union chapel power was the reality. The difference between the two was starkly demonstrated one year when I attended an NPA Council meeting to discuss the in-house wage situation before meeting with the unions for the annual pay negotiations. The previous year's deal had been for a 3 per cent increase, but it was immediately obvious that this had been more honoured in the breach than the observance.

'Right,' said Richard Marsh (later Lord Marsh), a former Labour minister who had gone on to become chairman of British Rail and who had subsequently been appointed chairman of the NPA. 'Can we go round the table so that members can report their in-house wage drift during the past year?' Wage drift was the difference between what the NPA had agreed with the national officers of the unions should be paid and what was actually paid to the work force by individual members of the NPA.

The captains of the newspaper industry reported one after another on life in the front line of the age-old management-union war, and they confessed that they had paid out more than the NPA agreement. Then the *Daily Telegraph* general manager, Hugh Lawson, owned up. 'I don't mind telling you that our wage drift is 12.5 per cent,' he said without a blush, and nobody present could bring themselves to cast the first stone in the greenhouse which was the reality of life with the chapels. With managements like this, it is little wonder that the Canadian entrepreneur Conrad Black hove into view and had little trouble in picking up the *Telegraph* titles from the controlling Berry family. But nobody was innocent of management malpractice, even when a company's own management men had to be sacrificed on the altar of expediency and production.

Among scores of examples, there was the time when the *Express* engineers of the AUEW went on strike – a particular problem because these were the men responsible for maintaining the foundry where the massive plates for the presses were cast. Here, in this industrial inferno, huge vats of molten metal were kept bubbling away at optimum temperatures 24 hours a day, 365 days of the year.

The tons of metal involved could not be allowed to cool and harden, for to heat them up again could take several days and even then many valves would be 'frozen' and immovable. No hot metal – no printing plates – no newspapers. Well aware of the repercussions of a strike, two engineering managers agreed to work on during the stoppage to ensure the worst did not happen. The two managers were AUEW men – in the crazy world of Fleet Street even managers had to be union members – and the end of the dispute was followed immediately by another one. The engineers refused to work with the managers who had volunteered to work. The managers' union cards were removed and the managers paid off. They were never allowed to work in the engineering world for the rest of their lives. This was the price they paid for being loyal to the company. The shop floor had won the day yet again.

The labour department was one of the hardest working groups of people in the entire company. (It was later renamed the industrial relations department to be in tune with the times. The name may have changed but it didn't make a blind bit of difference to the chapels who were the bane of the labour department's life.) The labour department's task was arduous, thankless and debilitating, even though the managers involved were men who had spent their lives on one side or other of the union fence. They were generally poachers turned gamekeepers – former senior chapel officials who had been persuaded to join the management team. Many must often have regretted their decision to change sides during the all-day meetings with chapel delegations as they attempted to cut the Gordian knots of ancient and impenetrable agreements while facing the rooted intransigence of their former comrades.

The labour department was involved in a permanent 'fire brigade' operation in which all too often the only action they could take was to turn the hosepipe of money on to the conflagration of the day. Their main job was to keep the plant running, but they were almost always in a no-win situation where they were trapped between the uncompromising demands of the unions and the equally rigid instructions of the chairman or managing director that under no circumstances should the production of the newspaper be imperilled and yet no extra money should be paid either.

The *Express* man with the impossible job of squaring the circle was the industrial relations director, Alan Bellinger. He was, and is, a genial man with immense experience of unions and negotiations, and I exempt him from the criticisms that can legitimately be made of spineless Fleet Street managements. For instance, it was he who led the charge during the Fleet Street revolution and achieved a staff reduction of 5000 once the legal and union shackles had been removed.

But in the dark days one of Alan's main jobs was to try to keep the unions and chapels away from the chairman and managing director. This was no easy task for the unions always wanted to arrange a meeting with the top dogs even over the most trifling of disputes. They had good reasons to do so for experience had taught them that if they could leapfrog the on-line management and put their case, laced with threats, to the top brass they could get away with the nearest thing to murder because the decision-making process could go no further.

The chapel officials knew that once past the labour department they were galloping to the winning post, for then it was the chairman or managing director who was put on the spot and had to make a decision or risk the paper. This was a position to be avoided at all costs. Settlements made by the top men, who often had been given a sketchy and hurried briefing on the current problem, could have horrendous spin-off effects. And it was the labour department which was left to unscramble the inevitable mess, and try to make sense of the madness.

For example, there was the time when the reel intake staff were playing merry hell with production by delaying the delivery of reels of newsprint from a seemingly endless queue of lorries. Jocelyn Stevens was managing director at the time and he decided that the situation was so critical that it demanded his intervention. Matching action to words, he proceeded to contact Alan Bellinger by getting on the internal telephone, a monstrous wooden 'squawk box', a relic of Beaverbrook days, with large levers to push down for instant contact and lights which flashed to indicate incoming messages. My heart usually sank when the light lit up showing that Jocelyn was on the line. On this occasion Alan was subject to a torrent of colourful language issuing from the box as Jocelyn demanded to know what the harassed industrial relations chief was doing to solve the crisis. Alan's explanations were cut when short Jocelyn came up with the final solution. 'Sack them, Bellinger!' he bellowed.

Bellinger was stunned by the instructions for he knew that the minimum consequences would be the loss of that day's *Daily Express* plus the loss of the hugely profitable *Sunday Express*. Nevertheless, he had been given his orders. Dismissal notices were hurriedly typed out as he summoned the father of the reel room intake chapel who was issued with the dismissal notices (including one for the FoC himself).

Within an hour Jocelyn was on the squawk box again. 'Have you sacked them?' he demanded. He was told that they had all been given their notices. Jocelyn erupted, 'Get them back, you fucking idiot,' he roared, 'or we'll lose the *Sunday Express.*'

A bemused, and increasingly anxious, Bellinger made his way to the reel intake area, wondering how to get out of this pickle and what on earth he could tell the chapel officials and their members. As Bellinger approached he could hear the rumble of a mass meeting in progress. The father of the chapel was in the process of telling his men that they had all been sacked. The mood was ugly. Bellinger pushed through the crowd and beckoned the FoC to one side. Quietly, and shamefacedly, he asked the union man, 'Could I have my dismissal letter back, please – the chairman says that I acted in far too precipitate a manner.' The FoC had Bellinger at his mercy, but to his credit, he appreciated the realities of the situation. 'I know what's going on,' he said, and passed the letters over.

Bellinger breathed a huge sigh of relief and returned to his office believing that he had performed a minor miracle. But no sooner had he returned than Jocelyn was back on the dreaded squawk box telling him to go along to see the chairman, Victor Matthews.

'How did you get them back, old boy?' asked Victor. Bellinger explained that he had taken the liberty of using the chairman's name and gave him the full details. 'Right oh, old boy,' said Victor amiably and once more Bellinger returned to his office. He had barely had time to sit down when he was greeted by the squawk box erupting into life yet again and Jocelyn's angry voice roaring at him: 'Don't ever use the chairman's name again! Do you hear – never!'

Not for the first time in his years as industrial relations director of the *Express*, Bellinger felt that sometimes life could be a real bitch.

Jocelyn had a love-hate relationship with the unions and they with him. One part of him hated the way they were able to keep a pistol to his head; another part wanted to be loved by them. This meant he was often on familiar terms with the union leaders and this familiarity was often reciprocated in spades.

Shortly after the Trafalgar House take-over, Jocelyn accompanied Nigel Broackes, chairman of Trafalgar House, and his wife to a smart racing event and began escorting them around the paddock. On the opposite side of the paddock Jocelyn spotted George Willoughby, secretary of the London branch of SOGAT, and a serious racing enthusiast. George was quite a character and a force to be reckoned with in his day although he was not known for his mental agility. Once, when one of his union officers was caught 'in flagrante' at union headquarters he accused the individual of being a 'dirty bugger' because he had been caught having 'verbal sex'.

Another time when I was providing drinks one evening in the boardroom for a ragtag of SOGAT officials, I was suddenly aware that George had removed his socks and was sitting with bare feet up on the boardroom table. At the same time he was flicking his mates in the face with a none too fresh sock. He also had a son who was a policeman and in meetings with Jocelyn would keep calling him a helicopter pilot and threaten that his son would come and arrest Jocelyn (presumably by landing his helicopter in the middle of Fleet Street).

This was the union chieftain whose attention Jocelyn attracted by bellowing 'George!' across the paddock. George duly trotted over, mackintosh tightly belted and a furled umbrella over his arm. 'Mr Broackes,' said Jocelyn, 'this is George Willoughby – he's the union branch secretary who controls the distribution of published material in London. George, this is Mr Broackes, the chairman of Trafalgar House which now owns Beaverbrook Newspapers.' George surveyed the party and peering through his thick glasses suddenly leant over, patted Mrs Broackes on her knicker line and said, 'Putting on a bit of weight, ain't you girl?'

I frequently met the composing room chapels, mainly because it was in that area that the most phenomenal earnings were taken home by piece workers who exploited unmercifully an ancient, anachronistic agreement whose origins were lost in the mists of time. This was the infamous London Scale of Prices, or London Piece Scale as it was formally known.

As its title implies, this curious arrangement applied in London only. Among other things, it dictated the price at which every single piece of type was paid for over a wide variety of rates, depending on the type size and style. Almost everything seemed to increase the applicable rate. Corrections increased the rate and even errors by the compositors added to their take home pay. In simple terms, a Linotype operator could make a mistake in a line of type, set it in the wrong measure, or misspell a word, and not only get paid for setting the wrong line but then get paid again for setting it correctly.

It is a measure of Fleet Street's industrial madness that failure not only went unpunished but that additional payments were made for making mistakes. Given this folly it was hardly surprising that 'mistakes' ran at a high level in the composing room with a large proportion of them being deliberately made.

There was absolutely no control by the company over this lunacy. The piece-work sectors – the Linotype operators and the case hands who still set the large headlines manually in movable type – would present the company with an overall bill at the end of each week, and they would then specify how much each of their members was to receive. The accounts department simply had to follow the chapel's instructions, deduct tax, pension contributions and national insurance and return the balance to the named individuals.

The monarch of all he surveyed in this hot metal kingdom was undoubtedly the man who revelled in the grand, if slightly sinister, title of the imperial father of the NGA composing chapels. His was a full-time job, even though he was paid by the company.

Thus, although he was on the company payroll, he never did a hand's turn on company business but instead devoted his considerable energies to creating as much mayhem and disruption for the company that was paying his wages – all in the interests of defending his members' interests.

Meetings with the imperial father generally meant that crunch time for the company was imminent. The imperial father was always attended by two members of each section within the composing room – the Linotype operators and the time hands (these were generally known as stone hands for their job was to make up the pages of type on the stone which in days gone by had been a simple slab of stone).

These acolytes always attended the imperial father's meetings because they didn't trust one another. So meetings with the imperial father were generally grim affairs.

Although, occasionally, they could be leavened with humour. I remember one time when I had called a meeting – the wages of the Linotype operators had once again gone through the roof – and I wanted to know how this had happened. I sent for the NGA and asked them to bring their bible – the piece book into which all charges under the London Piece Scale were entered. (No manager really understood the Piece Scale but we had to make a pretence of knowing.)

The imperial father, Dick Davies, attended by his court, came into my office with a broad grin on his face. This boded ill for me and the reason soon became clear.

Davies was holding a small, beautifully leather-bound volume which he passed to me with the words, 'This is from union records. Would you turn to page four and read it out to the assembled company?'

'What is it?' I asked nervously, for I felt that it would contain nothing to my advantage.

'It is the 1811 revision of the 1786 Piece Scale, the original agreement between the Masters and the Printers of the time,' he said. So I turned to page four and dutifully read out what was written:

'A Journeyman Printer, competent in the hand setting of Latin, Greek, Music and English, will receive the sum of £2 17s 6d per week by the agreement of the Masters.'

The trap was sprung. 'We've been working out,' said Davies, 'that with inflation we are being underpaid and we should be getting closer to £4000 a week.' But he said it, thank goodness, with a twinkle in his eye and the delegation fell about laughing. I suspect I would have had to challenge his members on their skills in the hand setting of Latin, Greek and Music (although it could be said that the London Piece Scale was Greek to almost everybody).

And it is worth bearing in mind that at the same time as the printers in 1811 were earning £2 17s 6d a week, the soldiers of Wellington's army and the sailors of the recently killed Admiral Nelson were building the British Empire and dying in their thousands for around 6d a week. Some things never change …

I remember a much more chilling meeting when I told the NGA that their claim would bankrupt the company. Their reply was brutal. Profits, they said, were nothing to do with them. Potential bankruptcy, too, was definitely a management concern and definitely not union business. It was shortly after this encounter that I learned one of the soundest lesson of trade union industrial relations. It came from a retired union official who had spent his life fighting – and generally winning – pay battles with the likes of me.

We were both at a splendid Maundy Thursday dinner dance in the heart of the City of London. (Maundy Thursday was the traditional night of revelry for the print workers dating back decades to the time when no newspapers were ever published on the following day, Good Friday. This tradition was upheld until the Wapping Revolution when newspapers went onto a 364 days a year production cycle.)

The NGA veteran was sitting at my table, and in the course of the genial conversation he suddenly said to me, 'Andrew, do you mind me saying something to you. Something as a young manager you must learn to come to terms with?' His tone of voice indicated that he obviously thought it was important, and I asked him to explain. 'It's simple,' he said. 'You and I can drink together, eat together, socialise together and even enjoy each other's company. But never forget that when we come to the negotiating table, our mandates are very different.' The dignified senior statesman of the NGA was spelling out the great 'them and us' divide which brought Fleet Street to its knees. Profits or bankruptcy was nothing to do with the unions. I never forgot his lesson.

There were, of course, many amusing moments, in the crazy world of the Fleet Street unions. For example, I was at a union dinner dance where the men had gathered to have a drink together in a group as men do on such occasions. Their wives or girlfriends were huddled together a little distance away.

In one of those momentary silences which suddenly happen at such events, a rather high, penetrating female voice was heard to remark, 'Isn't it terrible in this day and age our men are made to work six nights a week?'

The woman's husband was a foundryman who worked nineteen hours a week at most spread over a normal three, and occasional four, shifts a week. Poor woman – nobody knew where to look and no one felt obliged to enlighten her either.

For in those days men were paid cash wage packets. These were either delivered by hand to the various chapels or collected and signed for at the cashiers. One pay day, a foundryman approached the cashier's window holding a letter of authority from a sick colleague who was home in bed with a bad back. The man had never previously missed collecting his wage packet personally. Having checked the letter confirming that the foundryman could collect the sick man's pay packet, the cashier handed over the packet stuffed with notes and turned to go about his business.

'Hold on a minute,' said the foundryman, 'I want you to watch what I do.' He proceeded to remove a blank 'phoney' wage slip from his pocket. He then took out a pocket calculator and began filling in the slip, working out the figures as he went. He then opened the genuine packet and removed about half of the money, leaving the balance in the envelope. Enclosing the forged wage slip, he handed the packet back to the cashier and said, 'It's OK, you can now send it round to his wife.'

Members of another of the unions stole a barrel of ale from a well-known Fleet Street hostelry, no mean feat. The publican called the police, who carried out a search of the *Express* machine room without success. The culprits, NATSOPA machine-minders' assistants, had emptied the fire buckets round the walls and filled them with the contents of the barrel. No doubt if the police had discovered the beer in the fire buckets, the machine-minders' assistants would have put on an air of open-eyed innocence and claimed it was a miracle.

Negotiations with unions on new methods of working and new technology were always the most arduous of all. The not-so-hidden agenda at all such meetings was the undeniable fact that the print workers were the biggest bunch of reactionaries imaginable. They had good reason to be like this. The unions wanted almost everything to stay as it was, complete with their outrageous pay packets and short working hours. Their motto could well have been 'maintain the status quo', and if there were going to be any changes they would have to be to the advantage of the trade unions. Otherwise, the changes would simply never come about at all.

The stories of machinery costing millions of pounds being installed and never used are absolutely true. For instance, the *Telegraph* bought new presses in the 1950s but for 40 years they sat in the impressive grey stone *Telegraph* building, just along Fleet Street from the *Express*, and never turned out a single copy. Agreements for staffing the presses and paying the machine-minders and other chapels could never be reached despite strenuous efforts on the *Telegraph* management's part. When the part of the *Telegraph* building containing the machinery was eventually demolished in the late 1980s, the still 'new' presses were sold off for scrap metal. The *Telegraph* didn't learn their lesson, either. They bought in photo-composing equipment in the early 1980s which was only a year or two ahead of its time. But the result was the same – this equipment, too, stood idle until the building was pulled down.

I take no delight at the hapless *Telegraph*. The *Express* had its own horror stories.

Part of the small leap forward in the pre-Wapping new technology mini-revolution of the 1970s was the necessary upgrading of the foundry, the 'Dante's Inferno' department, which was a most unpleasant place to work in although it did have its amusing moments. I remember one chap who had a wooden leg. He fell asleep in a chair and some of the other men poured methylated spirit on to the oak appendage, then set fire to it. The man leaped to his feet yelling in panic. The rest of the men fell about, and for years talked about the day they 'burned old Bert down'.

In the foundry 48 lb metal printing plates were cast from a mixture of metals of extreme social unfriendliness, including lead. This material was poured at a constant 600 degrees Fahrenheit against a pre-

prepared papier mâché-type material known as a 'flong' – this was the size of one broadsheet page or two tabloid pages. Each press required two plates of each page, half cylindrical, to fit on to the printing press cylinder where it was firmly locked into place. Running twenty presses required vast numbers of such plates: 40 plates for each page, therefore a 64-page broadsheet newspaper would require 2560 plates for the first edition alone. Naturally, the plates were recycled, for the metals mixed to form the alloy in the plates were worth a tidy sum.

One hot summer's day a crowded lift from the foundry to the ground floor stuck half-way. Five, ten, fifteen minutes passed ... and as the trapped passengers grew more panicky and the heat rose, one foundryman, wearing a coat despite the heat, sank slowly to his knees in a corner of the lift. When, finally, the lift restarted and came to rest at the ground floor, the foundryman lay in a heap unable to move. He seemed to have suffered a 'turn'. His colleagues tried to lift him but he was a dead weight. This was hardly surprising. When his coat was removed it was found that he was carrying four curved metal plates, one on his chest, one on his back, one covering his bum and the other his crotch. It was discovered that he was making four or five trips a day to a metal dealer down in the East End and had the springs of his Ford Cortina estate specially strengthened to take the weight of his stolen goods. He didn't steal from the foundry again.

Up until the early 1970s much of the work in the foundry was done manually, which was hard, hot and dangerous to health; and foundrymen were not noted for their gentle disposition or co-operative attitude to management. Payments were frequently made to the turbulent foundry workers to keep them quiet, under a method known as dropping a shift payment or two 'in the bin' to be divvied up by the boys when the 'bin' was of sufficient size. This was a pretty crafty method of extortion which didn't affect the differentials with other NGA sections who would have been down like vultures if the gravy had been poured on to basic wages.

Suddenly mechanisation loomed. Some technical guru had been to the USA on a fact-finding trip, and had spotted a new method of automatic plate casting at some small upstate newspaper with one or so presses and tiny circulation. Known as the Woods 4/60, because the machine would cast four plates every 60 seconds using only one operator, it promised to be no less than a miracle to hard-pressed Fleet Street managements. Time proved that the Wood 4/60s certainly needed a miracle or two to work in the high pressure environment of a UK national newspaper. The machines were a nightmare.

First, the machines were wrongly installed, and never recovered from this dramatic birth. They broke down more frequently than it was possible to imagine, and with only three machines to cope with the entire requirements of so many presses, there were frequent periods of 'non production' when no newspapers would leave the building. Then when the presses began to run, deliveries would be late all over the country, presenting great sales opportunities to rival titles who had not gone in for this technical madness.

What an opportunity this all presented for the boys to line their pockets!

From the very beginning, the foundrymen had their eye on the main chance. Where previously six operators were needed in the old foundry, only one would be required with the Woods 4/60. The general view on the foundry shop-floor was that management just had to be joking. The NGA soon beat the management into the ground and negotiated probably the most obscene deal ever agreed by the company – a nineteen-hour week with thirteen weeks' holiday. This meant that these wonderful labour-saving devices saved no labour at all. There were 86 foundrymen before the Woods 4/60s were installed, and 86 foundrymen employed afterwards. Given a little bit of co-operation with your mates on rotas and you could work six months on and six months off and still receive your annual wages of £26,000, plus of course your share of the notorious 'bin'.

The 4/60s also presented the press operatives with a lucrative new opportunity, because every now and again the machines would produce a 'bad' plate, which didn't lock properly on to the press, so when the press gained speed, shrapnel suddenly started to fly. Although there were special metal guards to prevent injury, these incidents were regarded as very dangerous. Only the regular turning on the fire-hose of money turning on at very high pressure could remove the danger, get the press replated and the boys to return to work.

At least the Wood 4/60s worked after a fashion. We were not so lucky with the new printing presses. In the mid-1970s it was recognised that many of the older presses, the Goss machines, were long past their sell-by date (some of them were almost a hundred years old). The then Beaverbrook board decided to install the latest state-of-the-art version of the Ampress machine. They already had eight earlier versions of the Ampress press installed and running, and signed a deal to buy an additional three presses to be installed by contractors working for the US manufacturers. The problem with this second installation was, that unlike the first which was installed in a new building, the new line was to be built within the existing premises, and therefore fell under the jurisdiction of the unions.

The inevitable trouble started as soon as the contractors arrived to begin work, for the chapels were eager and ready for the fray. The first shots were fired by the electricians and their father of chapel, Ron Cowell. They claimed that the installation of the presses should be done by them and the fact that most newspaper electricians at the time could barely change a plug, far less install a new high-tech press, was entirely irrelevant.

As so often happened, a shoddy back-room deal was struck which involved paying the electricians' chapel some £50,000 just to turn a blind eye to the work being done by the contractors and to stop their bleating. This did not preclude, however, the electricians insisting that they should have the right to inspect the contractors' trade union membership cards to ensure that no 'scabs' were employed.

The engineers were next in line. The Ampress presses, they claimed, were 'machines' and everyone knew that machines needed engineers, even though their members' heavy engineering skills had not progressed much beyond their childhood sets of Meccano. So another claim was met by yet another cheapskate settlement and eventually the new presses were installed in the basement of the Fleet Street building.

Even worse was to come. As the work of installation neared completion, the management realised that there were no union agreements to run the presses on what had become known as the 'third line'. This news was the signal for every chapel in the building which could lay even the vaguest claim to being involved with the presses to pitch in and demand more and yet more money.

The new presses were ready to run by 1976 but they went down with the building when it was demolished in 1988, having never produced a single copy. Millions of pounds had been spent and many bank loans had to be serviced as the print unions pursued their insatiable greed for Fleet Street gold. It was this farcical, and ultimately suicidal, situation which was to prove the final straw that broke the back of Beaverbrook Newspapers and brought the final downfall of the empire which Beaverbrook had built.

19

WHY THE DINOSAURS DIED

I HAVE DESCRIBED how by the mid-1980s Fleet Street had been crippled by the tyranny of the print unions. Management was virtually helpless in their strangle grip. Management weakness and union avarice fed off each other. Even when managements tried to move forward, as Victor Matthews showed with the launch of the *Daily Star*, we were too often stymied. Millions of pounds' worth of new plant and machinery lay idle because of the failure of managements to win agreement to use them. Those in authority were helpless and the outlook seemed hopeless.

This was the appalling situation from which Fleet Street was rescued by the 'New Tech' revolution of the mid-1980s. It happened through a combination of three events, starting with the 'anti-union' industrial relations revolution pushed through parliament by Margaret Thatcher and her henchman Norman Tebbit. Suddenly, there was light at the end of the tunnel.

Eddie Shah in Warrington was the first to seize the opportunity to unshackle newspapers from the tyranny of the unions. Shah owned a small group of newspapers based in Stockport, Cheshire, but his ambitions knew few bounds and he burst into the sunny uplands of largely unfettered newspaper production with the launch of his *Today* newspaper in 1985.

The *Today* newspaper was revolutionary for it used web-offset presses and direct input computer technology to offer readers colour pictures and adverts throughout the paper, using previously unthinkable low staffing levels and therefore very low costs. The paper itself was not very good, either editorially or in terms of production quality. The colour pictures were generally grainy and blurred, and it betrayed its provincial origins at every turn. There were many teething troubles as the staff wrestled to cope with the new techniques and machinery which did not always live up to the high-tech advance publicity.

But Shah had launched and produced *Today* without any union agreements, and he defied the unions every night as his lorries emerged to run the gauntlet of pickets mounted by the print unions who instantly recognised the danger that *Today* represented both to their power and their enormous pay rates. By paving the way to both the union and colour revolutions which were to follow, Eddie Shah's newspaper (which was eventually swallowed up by the Murdoch empire) will always remain a landmark in the history of national newspapers. Shah kicked away the first bricks to make the hole in the wall through which ultimately the rest of Fleet Street rushed.

But the real breakthrough came when Rupert Murdoch, following the path pioneered by Shah, not only challenged the print unions but virtually destroyed them in the famous siege of Wapping.

What Shah had achieved, Murdoch had been itching to do for a long time. Like all other nationals, his popular titles, *The Sun* and *News of the World*, had also been the frequent victims of rabid union power, and suddenly the time was right for Murdoch to wreak his revenge.

Under conditions of paranoid but essential secrecy, Murdoch built and equipped a new, hi-tech printing plant at Wapping, using as a cover story that he might be launching a 24-hour London evening paper, the *London Post*, to challenge the *Evening Standard* and the *Evening News*. The unions waited complacently for him to come to them, and to strike the necessary deals as usual, naturally on their terms. Many meetings were held to negotiate manning levels, but the unions were intransigent about maintaining the ridiculous levels they were enjoying in Fleet Street.

The negotiations were a charade, of course. Murdoch had no intention of doing any more deals with them. He had suffered 'seventeen years of hell' in Fleet Street and there would be no inaction replays at Wapping. He went through the motions of talking with the NGA and SOGAT. He felt increasingly confident about his top-secret plan as he demanded from the unions terms for the *London Post* which included hitherto unheard-of demands for an end to closed shops, management's right to manage, dismissal for strikers and legally binding agreements – terms which the unions predictably rejected, just as they were expected to.

The only deal Murdoch struck was with Eric Hammond's electricians, the EETPU, with whom he signed an unprecedented agreement, the main point being that there would be no print unions at Wapping. All the jobs they had commandeered would be done by electricians who were signed up, as required, and bussed from as far away as Southampton. Murdoch's real secret weapon was his ATEX computer system which he brought in from the United States under heavy disguise.

After it was 'wired up' and tested at a secret warehouse in South London of identical dimensions to the Wapping editorial floor, it was smuggled into Wapping along with scores of Aussie and American techno-journalists who were flown in to produce type pages and pictures in readiness for the revolution, and to train the computer-illiterate journalists who still had not even the faintest clue of what was ahead of them. All this was being set up while the Murdoch titles were still being produced in Bouverie Street and Gray's Inn Road by journalists and hot metal printers who played like innocents in the late summer afternoon of the 'old' Fleet Street, all unknowing of their fate.

Murdoch now had in his hands virtually all the means of production to start the newspaper revolution, but the distribution of his newspapers was still crucially vulnerable. At that time, all newspapers were sent to their main destinations by rail and picked up from the stations by wholesalers. This system would put Murdoch at the mercy of the unions, for when the full extent of the Wapping revolution became obvious, it was inevitable that the militant rail unions would be asked by the print unions to show solidarity and support their trade union comrades. It was equally inevitable that the rail unions would respond to such a fundamental attack on the trades union movement.

Murdoch resolved this problem at a stroke with a move of breathtaking boldness which was to bring about yet another Fleet Street revolution. He decided to ditch the railways entirely and move his papers the length and breadth of Britain by truck. To achieve this he brought in 'my friends and partners in Australia', Thomas Nationwide Transport, or TNT, and put up £7 million towards the cost of buying 800 trucks and vans, and to help pay for the 2000 employees TNT hired. Today, more than ten years after Wapping, all national newspapers are delivered by truck. A business, which was worth hundreds of millions of pounds a year to British Rail, simply evaporated in a few short years. The print unions were not the only ones to kill the golden goose.

Meanwhile, the NUJ (National Union of Journalists) was instructing its members not to go to Wapping until negotiations with the print unions were concluded, but the printers themselves forced the issue. If they did nothing, there was no way that Murdoch could avoid paying them more than £40 million in redundancy payments whereas, if they went on strike, he could sack them with no compensation at all. The unions knew this, but they still had no conception of the scale of Murdoch's plans and believed he was bluffing. On Friday 24 January 1986 they called a strike for the following Monday. Murdoch's trap was set.

Now the gloves were off. The journalists were told they should report for work at Wapping the following day. The carrot was an immediate pay rise of £2000 a year plus free health insurance. And the stick? All those who refused would be considered to be on strike and instantly dismissed without compensation. The journalists were torn. They resented the ultimatum Murdoch had handed down, but they also knew that the computerised future of newspapers awaited them and they wanted to be part of it. Besides, what had the print unions ever done for them? Apart from stopping their words reaching the public on too many occasions over the years? Only eighteen months previously, NGA men had arrogantly walked through NUJ pickets in a previous editorial dispute.

Sun editor Kelvin McKenzie addressed his staff in his inimitable fashion. He urged his journalists to ignore the NUJ instructions and go to Wapping. 'What the NUJ has done for you would safely fit up a gnat's arse,' he declared. And the print unions? 'In a minute by minute industry when they've got you by the balls, you've got to listen. Well, they haven't got us by the balls any more.'

The Sun's journalists voted 100–8 to go to Wapping, and the *Sunday Times* and *Times* staff reluctantly followed suit. The *News of the World* and *Sunday Times* were already being prepared by a handful of journalists who had been slipped through the wire defences, and on the Saturday night Rupert Murdoch stood with his senior executives and pressed the button to start the presses. Shortly after 9 p.m. the first TNT lorries roared down the ramp at Wapping, and an hour later the scene was repeated at News International's Glasgow plant. That night, 25 January 1986, Murdoch papers published and distributed more than four million copies without any contribution at all from the traditional craft unions.

Another year was to pass before the unions finally bit the bullet; a year scarred by violence, militant picketing, injuries and even death. There was dissension and remorse among those who daily defied the pickets as they crept into Wapping in cars, buses, even armoured cars, amid a massive police presence.

But the days when the *Tyrannosaurus rex* of the print unions ruled were coming to an end. The dinosaurs were dying. The move to Wapping and that historic night of 25 January 1986 had changed newspapers for ever.

Nothing would ever be the same again.

So what conclusions do we come to about the final defeat of the print unions which had for so long held sway in the national newspaper world?

The first can only be summed up in the famous, and often incorrectly quoted words of Lord Acton:

'Power tends to corrupt and absolute power corrupts absolutely.'

The print unions had absolute power in Fleet Street. Through the years they had achieved an influence over their managements unmatched by any other group of unions in the trades union movement. The managements were ciphers.

Much of their power depended on the nature of the product they helped to produce – the daily or Sunday newspaper.

If miners go on strike, or rather when miners used to go on strike before the greed and stupidity of their unions, too, killed their own industry, there was still coal to be mined when they eventually returned to work.

When car workers downed tools, there was disruption, loss of production and another attack on the bottom line. But on their return, they could take up where they left off even though the company might have lost a few thousand cars in the process in the short term.

But newspapers are different. A day's newspaper production, even an issue's, once lost is lost forever. The newspaper is a transient thing. On the day the news, the views, the humour, the tragedy are relevant. If, due to industrial action it never appears, then it is worthless. It is dead before it is ever born.

It is this short-lived nature of newspapers which allowed the print unions to acquire such power over the years, and with the absolute power came the corruption which blinded them to reality and to the outside world which was rapidly changing around them without their noticing it.

They had created a world of their own, one which would have amazed their fellow trade unionists had they but known the full truth of the way the print union barons controlled and ran their industry.

It was not just a case of the outrageous pay packets, the claims or impenetrable arrangements like the London Scale of Prices. It was the web of rivalry and deceit among the individual and rival unions and the elaborate structure of ever-increasing insanities by which they aimed to perpetuate their power and prevent the real world from encroaching on their fantasy world. Not to mention the corruption which ran from top to bottom of most of the union structures and which finally began to corrode the souls of those who prospered from it and spread its tentacles into every corner of the industry.

So when the end came and the union dragon was slain by Murdoch, few, apart from those involved, shed a tear. They had brought their fate upon themselves.

Yet, don't get me wrong. Although as a senior manager in Fleet Street at the very height of trade union power I saw their abuses at first hand and suffered from their actions more than most, I did not rejoice at their defeat.

I recognised, above all, that I was witnessing the end of a tradition which, in its time, had purpose and nobility. Many of the print unions had descended from the medieval guilds and the printers of the Middle Ages. They had inherited a great tradition. The unions had a part to play in the protection of their members. Properly organised, the trade unions had, may still have, a role to play in the balance of power in industry.

But the key word is 'balance'. And somewhere along the way that balance was lost in Fleet Street. Instead, the scales of power were tipped decisively in one direction and the result was an intolerance and arrogance which in the end led to the downfall of the print unions.

I also did not rub my hands with glee because I knew many of the people involved personally, many of whom I was proud to call my friends. Most left with handsome redundancy payments and many made a success doing other things. Good luck to them.

But their world, the one they had grown up in, man and boy, was finished. The rank and file membership of the Fleet Street unions were not militant; few enjoyed the insane situations into which their leadership took them (although, being human, they didn't say 'no' to the money).

Yet in the end the average Fleet Street trade unionist was betrayed by his or her leadership – locally, at branch and nationally.

Had the leadership had more vision, more flexibility, even more cunning, they would have seen the way the wind was blowing in the world outside the narrow confines of Fleet Street. They would have made accommodation to the millions of pounds which Fleet Street managements were prepared to invest, indeed had invested, to try to take the industry into the next century. 'New' printing plants like those installed at the *Express* and *Telegraph* would not have gathered dust over the years and ended their days without producing a single copy. Whatever the sins of Fleet Street managements, and there were many, they were not afraid to invest in the future and many were broken in the process. Because in the end, whichever way they turned, they came up against the intransigence and negativity of the unions who wanted time to stand still, to take everything on offer and give nothing.

Even as I write, the union giant is stirring again. New Labour has indicated that there are strict limits to any changes which might be made to the trades union legislation introduced in the eighteen years of Conservative rule. Yet these are early days and the New Labour government could be in power in Westminster for ten years, possibly more. If, as Harold Wilson remarked, a week in politics is a long time, then five never mind ten years is a very, very long time.

The trades union movement, although currently a shadow of its former self, is still a power to be reckoned with. There are many in the movement still licking the wounds inflicted on them and seeking the revenge for the humiliation which they did so much to bring upon themselves.

The bad days of Fleet Street can never come back again, thank God. But I hope there will never come a day in any industry when any group, and I do not restrict it to the trades union movement, achieves a position in which it can wield absolute power on the scale the Fleet Street print unions enjoyed until it finally destroyed them.

AFTERWORD

IT WOULD BE SURPRISING if I did not gain some personal comfort from the fact that, since my departure from Express Newspapers in 1996, there have been three Managing Directors appointed by Clive Hollick and yet sales of the *Daily Express, Sunday Express* and *Daily Star* have continued to be damaged by the success of their competitors, mainly Associated Newspapers.

I have described my brief association with Hollick and the peremptory manner of his dismissal of me after what his own press release described as '24 years distinguished service'. Just before he gave me 'the chop' I was required to give a presentation to the great man and his entourage on what was needed to make the newspapers successful after the United Newspapers cash cow approach to the business. My reason for voting for the merger had been the belief that it offered a real chance for the Express to make progress in circumstances which saw it as a less dominant portion of the company of which it was part.

As a result for the previous regime's quest for profits at all cost, Express management had just put plans into place to save over £20 million in a full year but this cut no ice with Hollick. He said his philosophy was to give back half of any savings made but, from then on recent history did not count. It was to be a new beginning.

After my departure staff benefits were severely curbed; the staff bar and the executive restaurant were closed and, soon, no new entrants were allowed into the long established pension funds. His favoured 'battery hen' approach saw Hollick decimate the journalistic workforce and cram the Blackfriars Road building with all and sundry from various parts of the Empire. No heed was taken that a newspaper should have its own dedicated team to make it successful. The 'sausage machine' mentality of having staff working on any title at any time has been proven not to work but seven day publishing was Hollick's plan. That has never worked either and, after a period of plummeting sales for the *Express on Sunday*, the former, much loved and familiar title of the *Sunday Express* was brought back.

The Express titles were at their most successful in former years when they catered for their readers, not only the bean-counters. Customers often prized small elements of the papers – the crossword, the regionalised sports results, the named writers on a particular day. Jean Rook lifted sales on a Thursday because people bought that issue just for her piece and when John Junor departed for the *Mail on Sunday* some 80,000 sales were quickly lost by the *Sunday Express*. It is all about dedication to journalism and nurturing the right people.

It is also about good publicity because national newspapers are a big boys game and you cannot challenge a competitive opposition with one hand tied behind your back. Under United this tenet was not appreciated. United could not match the natural fervour of the former Express company which knew what it wanted to be; it could not really afford to own national newspapers and, deep down, was unhappy in the bullring competition which was the national press.

In November of each year, when I presented my business plan to the Board for the coming year, I tried hard to balance up the playing field with the opposition as best I could. The budgetary demands were rudimentary beancounting; the previous year's profits plus 15% was the starting point. Any ambitious plans to claw back lost ground were quickly dropped and often, one surmised, because several members of the board did not like, or did not want to pay for, the high profile that national newspaper ownership bestows. These men preferred low-risk, low profile ventures.

I was once told at a budget review meeting, 'Don't you realise, Andrew, that what you plan for one weekend's expenditure on television promotion is more that one year of profit for a small division?' This betrayed the need of the beancounters to please the City at all costs. Make acquisitions, please the institutions, were their mantras. This was understandable in a company the size of United Newspapers but the competitors of the Express titles worked to a different, more relevant, set of codes.

The much-revised budget, after acceptance by the beancounters, immediately stifled performance and development and caused frequent criticism from media correspondents, city analysts, and the UN Board itself. The fact that financial strictures meant we were playing uphill with eight men was seldom referred to.

I believed that the merger of United and MAI would allow a really competitive position to be created for the first time in years but, sadly, the standing of the Express titles since appears to have been eroded further under the new regime. Editorial is rightly the major cost centre of a newspaper. You risk the performance and credibility of your publication by employing low paid, inexperienced journalists. Quality comes from good writers, and from good exclusives bought for fair sums and with good judgement. Quality does not come by reducing freelance rates nor by employing a 'Hot Desk' policy. Quality is about people; newspapers are about people. Money saved at the *Express* has undoubtedly provided extra pages and an excellent Saturday magazine but no matter how big the can of beans it is the taste, the quality, that counts, and keeps people buying the cans! When *Today* closed I am sure its readers sampled the rival publications. The bulk certainly settled with the *Daily Mail* and left the current sales figures for the once proud Express titles tragically low.

Recent events have given credence to my chapters on the Jeffrey Archer libel trial and Brian Hitchen's relationship with Al Fayed. Many of the facts now emerging about Jeffrey Archer were known to us at the time, including the incident in Canada involving the suits and the emergence of a second girl claiming to have been paid for her sexual services. We were advised by our legal people not to go for character assassination because, should we lose it, it would simply aggravate the situation and could lead to exemplary damages. Frankly, the damages could not have been more exemplary, totalling £1.2 million including legal costs. Archer must have felt that his guardian angel was by his side when these facts were not introduced to the court.

What of the future? Rumours abound that the Express titles are up for sale and, indeed, I was recently asked to comment on their value by one interested group. My response was that I felt the value was probably restricted to good will as there do not appear to be significant tangible assets. I have also been asked whether the *Daily Star* could be bought but feel that the costs which would accompany this title probably rules out such a purchase. I cannot imagine Express Newspapers selling for what might be a more realistic independent value. Even the 'jewel in the crown' – the valuable WestFerry Printers – is 50 per cent owned by the *Daily Telegraph*.

I still believe there is a future for the Express titles but it will take dedicated newspaper proprietorship controlling the beancounters to make that happen.

INDEX